**pioneers
of modern
design**

To
T.B., T.B., W.B., W.A.C.,
W.G.C., J.P. *and* D.F., P.S.F.,
P. *and* E.G., H.R., F.M.W.,
the A.A.C., *the* C.I.
in gratitude

Nikolaus Pevsner

pioneers
of modern
design

from william morris to walter gropius

The Museum of Modern Art   New York

Contents

Foreword to the First Edition

Most of the preparatory work for this book was done during the years 1930–32. I held a class on the architecture of the nineteenth and twentieth centuries at Göttingen University in 1930, and then published, in the *Göttingische Gelehrte Anzeigen* of 1931, a short preliminary account of the parts played by the most important architects in the development of the Modern Movement.

However, as far as books on the subject are concerned, this is, if I am not mistaken, the first to be published. I am well aware of its shortcomings, and shall be grateful to anybody who may be able to draw my attention to sins of omission or of commission.

I did not know of P. Morton Shand's excellent articles in the *Architectural Review* of 1933, 1934, 1935 until I had almost finished my research. The fact that our conclusions coincide in so many ways is a gratifying confirmation of the views put forward in this book.

I feel greatly indebted to Geoffrey Baker, Katharine Munro, and Alec Clifton-Taylor, who tried to eliminate from my text the worst clumsiness of a foreign style. Yet I am afraid it is still badly lacking in that supple precision which distinguishes well-written English.

I also want to place on record my gratitude to my mother, Frau Annie Pevsner, who used a time of unwelcome leisure for transforming an illegible into a readable and printable manuscript, and to Mr. Richard de la Mare who with great kindness and understanding dealt with all matters of layout, printing and illustration.   NIKOLAUS PEVSNER

London, May, 1936

Foreword to the Second Edition

The Museum of Modern Art has increased the scope of this book considerably by raising the total number of illustrations from 84 to 137; I have tried to improve the text by corrections, where I had made mistakes, and by additions which vary in length from a line to a virtual re-writing of a whole chapter. For suggestions as to what should be altered and added I wish to thank Philip Johnson, Edgar Kaufmann Jr., Henry-Russell Hitchcock, and Alfred H. Barr, Jr. But my greatest gratitude is to Herwin Schaefer who has followed the book untiringly through all its stages from manuscript to printed page and never ceased to improve it by queries, checking and research.

London, December, 1948

Theories of Art from Morris to Gropius

"Ornamentation," says Ruskin, "is the principal part of architecture." It is that part, he says in another place, which impresses on a building "certain characters venerable or beautiful, but otherwise unnecessary." Sir George Gilbert Scott amplified this surprising statement when he recommended to architects the use of the Gothic style, because its "great principle is to decorate construction."[1]

How this basic doctrine of nineteenth-century architectural theory worked out in practice, could not be shown more convincingly than by retelling the story of the new British Government offices in Whitehall, London, as erected by Scott between 1868 and 1873. The following are the facts as told by Sir George. His original plans were in the Gothic style. He writes: "I did not aim at making my style 'Italian Gothic'; my ideas ran much more upon the French, to which for some years I had devoted my chief study. I did, however, aim at gathering a few hints from Italy. . . . I mean a certain squareness and horizontality of outline. . . . I combined this . . . with gables, high-pitched roofs and dormers. My details were excellent, and precisely suited to the purpose." In spite of this, Scott did not win the first prize in the competition, partly because Lord Palmerston thoroughly disliked medieval styles. Scott comments: "I did not fret myself at the disappointment, but when it was found, a few months later, that Lord Palmerston had coolly set aside the entire results of the competition, and was about to appoint Pennethorne, a non-competitor, I thought myself at liberty to stir." And stir he did, so that in the end he was appointed architect to the new building. However, he was not able to dissuade the Government from its predilection for the Italian Renaissance. What followed was described by Lord Palmerston as the battle of the Gothic and Palladian styles. He saw no insurmountable difficulty. He sent for Scott and told him "in a jaunty way that he could have nothing to do with the Gothic style, and that," continues Scott, "though he did not want to disturb my appointment, he must insist on my making a design in the Italian style, which he felt sure I could do quite as well as the other." Lord Palmerston was evidently right, for, after long arguments, Scott promised "an Italian design." But still he hoped that Renaissance could be avoided. He altered the front of his building, and now it was "in the Byzantine of the early Venetian palaces . . . toned into a more modern and usable form." In vain, for the Prime Minister wanted "the ordinary Italian," and he would have it. He called the new plans "neither one thing nor t'other — a regular mongrel affair," and threatened to cancel Scott's appointment. After that, for the sake of his family and his reputation, Sir George "in sore perplexity" decided to "swallow the bitter pill." He "bought some costly books on Italian architecture and set vigorously to work" to invent an Italian façade "beautifully got up in outline."[2]

The campaign of William Morris' lifetime was directed against the complete lack of feeling for the essential unity of architecture which made this comedy possible. When his impressionable nature began to react to buildings, fine art, and industrial art, almost all contemporary building which surrounded him, as a youth in London and as a student at Oxford, was either feeble or crude in design; and practically all industrial art vulgar and overloaded with ornament. Examples will be given later. Responsible for this state of affairs were the Industrial Revolution and — less known but equally important — the theory of esthetics created since 1800. The part played by the Industrial Revolution is to be discussed in Chapter 2. It is sufficient here to say that manufacturers were, by means of new machinery, enabled to turn out thousands of cheap articles in the same time and at the same cost as were formerly required for the production of one well-made object. Sham materials and sham technique were dominant all through industry. Skilled craftsmanship, still so admirable when Chippendale and Wedgwood were at work, was replaced by mechanical routine. Demand was increasing from year to year, but demand from an uneducated and debased population, living a slave-life in filth and penury.

The artist withdrew in disgust from such squalor. It was not for him to work for the needs of those classes, to condescend to the taste of the majority of his fellow men, to meddle with the "Arts Not Fine." During the Renaissance, artists had first learned to consider themselves superior beings, bearers of a great message. Leonardo da Vinci wanted the artist to be a scientist and a humanist, but by no means a craftsman. When Michelangelo was asked why he had portrayed one of the Medicis in the Medici Chapel beardless, though he had worn a beard in life, he answered: "Who, in a thousand years, will know what he looked like?" However, this attitude of artistic presumption remained exceptional until the end of the eighteenth century. Schiller was the first to form a philosophy of art which made the artist the high priest in a secularized society. Schelling took this up, and Coleridge, Shelley and Keats followed. The artist is no longer a craftsman, no longer a servant, he is now a priest. Humanity may be his gospel, or beauty, a beauty "identical with truth" (Keats), a beauty that is "the completest conceivable unity of life and form" (Schiller). In creating, the artist makes conscious "the essential, the universal, the aspect and expression of the indwelling spirit of Nature" (Schelling). Schiller assures him: "The dignity of Mankind is laid into thy hands," and compares him to a king — "both living on the summits of Mankind." The inevitable consequence of such adulation became more and more visible as the nineteenth century unfolded. The artist began to despise utility and the public (Keats: "Oh sweet fancy! let her loose; Everything is spoilt by use"). He shut himself off from the real life of his time, withdrawing into his sacred circle and creating art for art's, art for the artist's, sake. Concurrently the public lost understanding of his personal, outwardly useless utterances. Whether he lived like a priest or lived a *vie de Bohème,* he was ridiculed by most of his contemporaries, and extolled by only a small set of critics and wealthy connoisseurs.

But there had been a time when nothing of all that existed. In the Middle Ages the artist was a craftsman, proud of executing any commission to the best of his ability. Morris was the first artist (not the first thinker, for Ruskin had preceded him) to realize how precarious and decayed the social foundations of art had become during the centuries since the Renaissance, and especially during the years since the Industrial Revolution. He had been trained as an architect and as a painter, first in the Gothic studio of Street, and then in the circle of the Pre-Raphaelites. But when, in 1857, he had to furnish his first studio in London, the thought struck him that before one can settle down to paint elevating pictures, one must be able to live in appropriate surroundings, must have a decent house, and decent chairs and tables. Nothing was obtainable that could possibly satisfy him. This was the situation which all of a sudden awakened his own personal genius: if we cannot buy solid and honest furniture, let us make it ourselves. So he and his friends set out to build chairs "such as Barbarossa might have sat in" and a table "as heavy as a rock" (Rossetti). The same experiment was repeated when Morris had a house built for his wife and himself, the famous Red House at Bexley Heath. Ultimately, in 1861, instead of forming a new exclusive brotherhood of artists, such as the Pre-Raphaelite Brotherhood had been, and such as he had wished to found when he was studying at Oxford, Morris made up his mind to open a firm, the firm of Morris, Marshall & Faulkner, Fine Art Workmen in Painting, Carving, Furniture and the Metals. This event marks the beginning of a new era in Western art.

The fundamental meaning of Morris' firm and Morris' doctrine is clearly expressed in the thirty-five lectures which he delivered between 1877 and 1894 on artistic and social questions.[3] His point of departure is the social condition of art which he saw around him. Art "has no longer any root."[4] The artists, out of touch with everyday life, "wrap themselves up in dreams of Greece and Italy . . . which only a very few people even pretend to understand or be moved by."[5] This situation must seem exceedingly dangerous to anyone concerned with art. Morris preaches: "I don't want art for a few, any more than education for a few, or freedom for a few,"[6] and he asks that great question which will decide the fate of art in our century: "What business have we with art at all unless all can share it?"[7] So far Morris is the true prophet of the twentieth century, the father of the Modern Movement. We owe it to him that an ordinary man's dwelling-house has once more become a worthy object of the architect's thought, and a chair, a wallpaper, or a vase a worthy object of the artist's imagination.

However, this is only one half of Morris' doctrine. The other half remained committed to nineteenth-century style and nineteenth-century prejudices. Morris' notion of art derives from his knowledge of medieval conditions of work, and is part and parcel of nineteenth-century "historicism." Proceeding from Gothic handicraft, he defined art simply as "the expression by man of his pleasure in labor."[8] Real art must be "made by the people and for the people, as a happiness for the maker and the user."[9] The pride in artistic genius and some special form of inspiration, which he saw in all the art of his time, was therefore abhorrent to him. "That talk of inspiration is sheer nonsense" he said; "there is no such thing: it is a mere matter of craftsmanship."[10]

It is obvious that such a definition of art removes the problem from esthetics into the wider field of social science. In Morris' mind, "it is not possible to dissociate art from morality, politics and religion."[11] Here, above all, he proves a faithful follower of the Pre-Raphaelites and of Ruskin. His socialism is the necessary outcome of this attitude. He denounces the social structure of his age because it is evidently fatal to art. "Art . . . will die out of civilization, if the system lasts. That in itself does to me carry with it the condemnation of the whole system."[12] Thus Morris' socialism is far from correct according to the standards of the later nineteenth century: there is more in it of Thomas More than of Karl Marx. His main question is: how can we recover a state of things in which all work would be "worth doing" and at the same time "of itself pleasant to do?"[13] He looks backward, not forward, backward into the times of the Icelandic Sagas, of Cathedral building, of Craft Guilds. One cannot, from his lectures, obtain a clear view of what he imagined the future to be. "The whole basis of Society . . . is incurably vicious," he wrote.[14] Hence it was sometimes his only hope "to think of barbarism once more flooding the world . . . that it may once again become beautiful and dramatic withal."[15] And yet when, partly as a consequence of his own socialist propaganda, riots began in London and revolution seemed for a moment not unlikely, he recoiled and gradually withdrew back into his world of poetry and beauty.

This is the decisive antagonism in Morris' life and teaching. His work, the revival of handicraft, is constructive; the essence of his teaching is destructive. Pleading for handicraft alone means pleading for conditions of medieval primitiveness, and first of all for the destruction of all the devices of civilization which were introduced during the Renaissance. This he did not want; and since, on the other hand, he was unwilling to use any post-medieval methods of production in his workshops, the consequence was that all his work was expensive work. In an age when practically all objects of everyday use are manufactured with the aid of machinery, the products of the artist-craftsman will be bought by a narrow circle only. While Morris wanted an art "by the people and for the people," he had to admit that cheap art is impossible because "all art costs time, trouble and thought."[16] He thus created art — though now applied art, and no longer the nineteenth-century art of the easel-picture — which was also accessible to a few connoisseurs only, or, as he once expressed it himself, art for "the swinish luxury of the rich."[17] No doubt Morris' art has in the end beneficially affected commercial production in many trades, but that is precisely what he would have hated, because the diffusion of his style on a large scale involved reintroducing the machine, and thereby expelling once more the "joy of the maker." The machine was Morris' arch-enemy: "As a condition of life, production by machinery is altogether an evil."[18] Looking forward to barbarism, he certainly hoped for machine-breaking, though in his late speeches he was careful (and inconsistent) enough to admit that we ought to try to become "the masters of our machines" and use them "as an instrument for forcing on us better conditions of life."[19]

Morris' attitude of hatred towards modern methods of production remained unchanged with most of his followers. The Arts and Crafts Movement brought a revival of artistic craftsmanship, not of industrial art. Walter Crane (1845–1915) and C. R. Ashbee (1863–1942) may be taken as representatives of this. Walter Crane, the most popular of the disciples of Morris, did not go one step beyond the doctrine of his master. To him, as to Morris, "the true root and basis of all Art lies in the handicrafts."[20] His aim, therefore, just like Morris', is "to turn our artists into craftsmen and our craftsmen into artists."[21] Moreover, he agrees with Morris in the conviction that "genuine and spontaneous art . . . is a pleasurable exercise,"[22] and is led by such premises to a romantic socialism identical with that of Morris. The same conflict which was pointed out in Morris' doctrine is to be found in Crane. He too is compelled to admit that "cheapness in art and handicraft is well-nigh impossible" because "cheapness as a rule . . . can only be obtained at the cost of the . . . cheapening of human life and labor."[23] Crane's attitude towards machine production also corresponds to Morris'. His dislike of "the monsters of our time clad in plate-glass [and] cast-iron"[24] — Ruskin had been the first to inveigh against railway stations and the Crystal Palace — is tempered only by the consideration that machinery may be necessary and useful as "the servant and labor-saver of man" for a "real saving of labor, heavy and exhausting labor."[25]

Ashbee was certainly a more original thinker and more energetic reformer than Crane.[26] Proceeding also from Ruskin and Morris in his belief that "the constructive and decorative arts are the real backbone" of any artistic culture, that every object ought to be "produced under pleasurable conditions,"[27] and that therefore art for workaday use cannot be cheap, he surpasses Morris in that he links up the problems of workshop-reconstruction and of small holdings. His Guild and School of Handicraft, founded in 1888, was removed in 1902 from the East End of London to Chipping Campden in the Cotswolds. While this aspect of his work and doctrine is even more "medievalist" than the teaching of Morris, there is another side to his doctrine which seems genuinely progressive. At the time of the Guild his attitude towards machine production was still almost that of Morris and Crane. "We do not reject the machine" he wrote; "we welcome it. But we desire to see it mastered."[28] Within the next few years, partly perhaps as a consequence of the hopeless struggle of the Guild against modern methods of manufacturing, he broke away from what he now called Ruskin's and Morris' "intellectual Ludditism,"[29] and the first axiom of his last two books on art is that "Modern civilization rests on machinery, and no system for the encouragement or the endowment of the teaching of the arts can be sound that does not recognize this."[30]

In pronouncing this axiom, Ashbee has abandoned the doctrine of the Arts and Crafts and adopted one of the basic premises of the Modern Movement. But with him it was only adopting, and not creating. His foremost title to fame remains the Campden experiment, an attempt to revive handicraft and husbandry far from the centers of modern life. The true pioneers of the Modern Movement are those who from the outset stood for machine art. As forerunners, of a still somewhat transitional character, two contemporaries of Morris may be quoted, Lewis F. Day (1845–1910) and John Sedding (1837–91). Day, a well-known industrial designer of his time, wrote as one who prefers a life in the real world to dreams of a medieval and idyllic existence. In discussing the ornament of the future, he said in 1882: "Whether we like it or no, machinery and steam-power, and electricity for all we know, will have something to say concerning the ornament of the future." He said it would be useless to resist this fact, for it was "practically settled by the public that they want machine-work. . . . We may protest that they have chosen unwisely, but they will not pay much heed to us."[31] And Sedding, perhaps the most original church architect of the late Gothic Revivalist school, who became a pupil of Street just two years after Morris had left him, gave the same advice in 1892: "Let us not suppose that machinery will be discontinued. Manufacture cannot be organized upon any other basis. We had better clearly recognize this . . . rather than rebel against the actual and the inevitable."[32]

However, there is still an immense difference between this hesitating acknowledgment of machinery and the wholehearted welcome which it received in the writings of the leaders of the next generation. Not one of them was English: England's activity in the preparation of the Modern Movement came to an end immediately after Morris' death. The initiative now passed to the Continent and the United States, and, after a short intermediate period, Germany became the center of progress. English writers have not failed to acknowledge this fact;[33] but hardly anybody has tried to explain it. One reason may be this: so long as the new style had been a matter which in practice concerned only the wealthier class, England could foot the bill. As soon as the problem began to embrace the people as a whole, other nations took the lead, nations that lived no longer, or had never lived, in the atmosphere of the *ancien régime,* nations that did not accept or did not know England's educational and social contrasts between the privileged classes and those in the suburbs and the slums.

The new gospel was first preached by poets and writers. Walt Whitman in his odes and Zola in his novels are carried away by the overwhelming marvels of modern civilization and modern industry. The first architects to admire the machine and to understand its essential character and its consequences on the relation of architecture and design to ornamentation were two Austrians, two Americans and a Belgian: Otto Wagner (1841–1918), Adolf Loos (1870–1933), Louis Sullivan (1850–1924), Frank Lloyd Wright (born 1869) and Henry van de Velde (born 1863). To these five one Englishman should be added, Oscar Wilde (1856–1900), although his occasional praise of machine beauty may be only one of many laborious efforts at *épater le bourgeois.* He said in a lecture of 1882: "All machinery may be beautiful, when it is undecorated even. Do not seek to decorate it. We cannot but think all good machinery is graceful, also, the line of the strength and the line of the beauty being one."[34]

Van de Velde, Wagner, Loos and Wright were decisively stimulated in their thoughts by England. Wright's manifesto was read at Hull House in Chicago, Wagner expressed his great admiration of the comfort and cleanness of English industrial art,[35] Loos said explicitly: "The center of European civilization is at present in London,"[36] and his early criticism was to a large extent passionate support of the exhibitions of modern English objects arranged by the Österreichisches Museum in Vienna. And from van de Velde's writings the following statement may be quoted: "The seeds that fertilized our spirit, evoked our activities, and originated the complete renewal of ornamentation and form in the decorative arts, were undoubtedly the work and the influence of John Ruskin and William Morris."[37]

Only Louis Sullivan, whose *Ornament in Architecture* is the earliest of these manifestoes of a new style, seems to have been independent of England. In his distant Chicago, where metropolitan architecture at that time meant New York and Boston and, further afield, Paris, he worked out entirely on his own the theory which found its final form in the *Kindergarten Chats* of 1901–02.[38] In *Ornament in Architecture* Sullivan stated already in 1892 that "ornament is mentally a luxury, not a necessary," and that "it would be greatly for our esthetic good, if we should refrain entirely from the use of ornament for a period of years, in order that our thought might concentrate acutely upon the production of buildings well formed and comely in the nude."[39]

This approval of the unadorned surface was in itself not new. It had already been said by Crane in 1889 that "plain materials and surfaces are infinitely preferable to inorganic or inappropriate ornament,"[40] and one year after Sullivan, Charles F. Annesley Voysey wrote that "discarding the mass of useless ornaments" would be healthy and desirable.[41] But just as Voysey, in spite of such suggestions, has been one of the most important representatives of the evolution of ornament between Morris and the twentieth century, so Sullivan was in fact just as much a revolutionary in his ornament as in his use of plain, smooth surfaces. In his same paper of 1892, he stated that "organic ornament" should be the stage to follow the purge of all ornament which had to come first.

Sullivan's own decorative motifs belong to the species known as *Art Nouveau*. So do those of van de Velde who, in his lectures between 1894 and 1900,[42] pronounced — independently without doubt — the same faith in a type of ornament which would be able to express symbolically "by means of pure structure . . . joy, lassitude, protection, etc.,"[43] and in the machine as a stimulus to the achievement of a new beauty. Van de Velde showed his audience that a great deal of the English Arts and Crafts had remained a pastime of highly sensitive artists for highly sensitive connoisseurs, and therefore was not much healthier than the exquisite and decadent writing of Huysmans. He contrasted Morris' art, which never broke away from reminiscences of the Gothic centuries, with his own new doctrine of the beauty inherent in machines. "The powerful play of their iron arms," he exclaimed, "will create beauty, as soon as beauty guides them."[44] This statement dates from 1894 (1890?). Six years later van de Velde added more explicitly: "Why should artists who build palaces in stone rank any higher than artists who build them in metal?"[45] "The engineers stand at the entrance to the new style."[46] Engineers are "the architects of the present day."[47] What we need is "a logical structure of products, uncompromising logic in the use of materials, proud and frank exhibition of working processes."[48] A great future is prophesied for iron, steel, aluminum, linoleum, celluloid, cement.[49] As to the appearance of objects in the house, van de Velde pleads for "that lost sense of vivid and strong, clear colors, vigorous and strong forms, and reasonable construction,"[50] and praises the new English furniture for its "systematic discarding of ornament."[51]

Precisely this was to be Adolf Loos's gospel. He had been trained as an architect, first in Dresden and then in the United States.[52] Coming back to Vienna in 1896, he was shown a small newly published book by Vienna's most progressive architect, Otto Wagner.[53] The book was based on Wagner's Inaugural Lecture at the Art Academy, in 1894, and its doctrine was in many respects similar to van de Velde's. "The only possible departure for artistic creation is modern life."[54] "All modern forms must be in harmony with . . . the new requirements of our time."[55] "Nothing that is not practical can be beautiful."[56] So Wagner foresaw a "coming Naissance"[57] and what is more astonishing, pointed out as some of the characteristics of that future style "horizontal lines such as were prevalent in Antiquity, table-like roofs, great simplicity and an energetic exhibition of construction and materials."[58] Needless to say, he too was passionately in favor of iron.

Adolf Loos wrote his first essays for newspapers and periodicals in 1897 and 1898.[59] Attacking the Viennese *Art Nouveau* style, known as the style of the *Sezession* which was just then at its height, he pointed out: "The lower the standard of a people, the more lavish are its ornaments. To find beauty in form instead of making it depend on ornament is the goal towards which humanity is aspiring."[60] For pure beauty in an individual work of art is to Loos "the degree to which it attains utility and the harmony of all parts in relation to each other."[61] The engineers he regards therefore as "our Hellenes. From them we receive our culture."[62] And he is consistent enough to call the plumber (the term being used in the general American sense) "the quartermaster of culture, i.e. of the kind of culture which is decisive today."[63]

Only a few years later similar views were expressed with equally strong conviction, though in a more comprehensive and sweeping style, by Sullivan's greatest pupil, Frank Lloyd Wright, who in 1901 read a manifesto on *The Art and Craft of the Machine*.[64] It begins straightaway with a panegyric on our "age of steel and steam . . . the Machine Age, wherein locomotive engines, engines of industry, engines of light or engines of war or steamships take the place works of Art took in previous history."[65] Wright enthusiastically admires the new "simplified and etherealized" rhythm of future buildings, where — an amazing prophecy — "space is more spacious, and the sense of it may enter into every building, great or small."[66] In such an age the painter or the poet does not count for much. "Today, we have a Scientist or an Inventor in the place of a Shakespeare or a Dante."[67]

But if Wright speaks of today, he means the twentieth century as it could be and ought to be, and not as it appeared in 1901. The many disgraceful things perpetrated by machines are, according to Wright, the fault not of the machine but of the designers. For "the machine has noble possibilities, unwillingly forced to this degradation . . . by the Arts themselves."[68] Hence one can be in no doubt as to the victory in the battle between the artist, in the old sense, and the machine. The machine is a "relentless force" bound to discomfit the "handicraftsmen and parasitic artists."[69] It sounds like a deliberate challenge to Morris' "Art will die out of civilization, if the system lasts. That in itself does to me carry with it the condemnation of the whole system," when Frank Lloyd Wright, looking at Chicago's overwhelming silhouette and lights by night, exclaims: "If this power must be uprooted that civilization may live, then civilization is already doomed."[70] And Wright's belief in the machine is so strong that he foresees a possible salvation for the craftsman in his humbly learning from the machine. "Rightly used," he says, "the very curse machinery puts upon handicraft should emancipate the artists from temptation to petty structural deceit and end this wearisome struggle to make things seem what they are not and never can be."[71]

So Wright's position in 1901 was almost identical with that of the most advanced thinkers on the future of art and architecture today. However, this theory remained isolated in America for a long time. And it is an indisputable fact that in most European countries as well, those who pleaded for a new style of the century found very little response before the First World War. This was for instance the case with Anatole de Baudot who, as early as 1889, said: "A long time ago the influence of the architect declined and the engineer, *l'homme moderne par excellence,* is beginning to replace him";[72] and it was also the case with H. P. Berlage (1856–1934) in Holland who, in two articles in 1895 and 1896, recommended to the architect not to think in terms of style while designing buildings. Only thus, he said, can real architecture comparable to that of the Middle Ages be created, architecture as a "pure art of utility."[73] Such architecture he visualized as *"the* art of the 20th century," and it should be noted that the century to him was to be one of Socialism.[74]

To have achieved a wide movement promoting these new ideas, is undeniably the merit of German architects and writers. The movement which they fostered proved strong enough to yield a universal style of thinking and building, and not merely some revolutionary sayings and deeds of a few individuals.

The man who acted as a connecting link between the English style of the nineties and Germany was Hermann Muthesius (1861–1927) who, from 1896 till 1903, was attached to the German embassy in London for research on English housing. Since *Art Nouveau* had hardly diverted English domestic architecture from the sound and slow course of its evolution, Muthesius came back a convinced supporter of reason and simplicity in building and art. Soon he became the acknowledged leader of a new tendency towards *Sachlichkeit,* which followed the short blossom-time of *Art Nouveau* in Germany. The untranslatable word *sachlich,* meaning at the same time pertinent, matter-of-fact, and objective, became the catchword of the growing Modern Movement.[75] "Reasonable *Sachlichkeit*" is what Muthesius praises in English architecture and crafts,[76] "perfect and pure utility" is what he demands from the modern artist. And since today only machine-made objects are "produced according to the economic nature of the age," they alone can be taken into consideration where the problem is the creation of a new style, a *Maschinenstil.*[77] If we want to see existing manifestations of this new style, we are once more invited to look at "railway stations, exhibition halls, bridges, steamships, etc. Here we are faced with a severe and almost scientific *Sachlichkeit,* with abstinence from all outward decoration, and with shapes completely dictated by the purposes which they are meant to serve." Hence future progress can be imagined only in the direction of strict *Sachlichkeit* and a discarding of all merely "tacked-on" decoration. Buildings or objects for use that are created on such lines will display "a neat elegance which arises from suitability and . . . conciseness."[78]

By pronouncing such ideas, still unfamiliar in Germany, Muthesius soon became the center of a group of congenial spirits. Of paramount importance, owing to the echo which he found among the bourgeoisie listening to his lectures and reading his pamphlets, was Alfred Lichtwark (1852–1914), art historian and director of the Hamburg Gallery. He was a teacher by nature, obsessed with the purest passion for education. The rapid development of art education in the widest sense of the word, which has taken place in the German elementary schools and secondary schools since the beginning of the new century, is largely due to Lichtwark's efforts. His campaign in favor of *Sachlichkeit* started even earlier than Muthesius'. In the lectures which he delivered between 1896 and 1899, and which are full of praise for England, he pleaded for practical, unadorned furniture in "smooth, polished, light forms" convenient to housewives, for *sachliche Schönheit,* for wide horizontal windows and "floods of light," and for fresh flowers in the rooms.[79]

Three more quotations may be taken from the writings of other partisans, the first from Hermann Obrist, one of the most original artists of the German *Art Nouveau,* the second from Wilhelm Schäfer, a well-known writer and poet, the third from Friedrich Naumann, a politician of importance in the development of social reforms and democracy in pre- and post-First World War Germany. Obrist wrote in 1903 of steamers and "the beauty in the powerful sweep of their colossal yet quiet contours . . . their wonderful utility, their neatness, smoothness and shine." A look into the engine-room makes him feel "almost intoxicated."[80] Wilhelm Schäfer vividly recommends the *sachliche Ausbildung* of all forms; this would necessarily lead to a modern style for all products, just as it has done in machines and iron bridges.[81] As to Friedrich Naumann, his main interest was in the social aspects of architecture and art. This led him to an early appreciation of the machine. Exactly like Muthesius, and no doubt inspired by him, Naumann speaks of "ships, bridges, gasometers, railway stations, market halls, exhibition halls" as "our new buildings." He calls "building in iron the greatest artistic experience of our time," because "here there is not the application of art to construction, no stuck-on decoration, no frills. Here is creation for use . . . here are as yet inexpressible possibilities. All our notions of space, of weight and support are changed."[82]

Naumann was a personal friend of Karl Schmidt (died in 1948) who, as a trained cabinetmaker, had started a furniture workshop at Dresden in 1898. In this shop he employed from the beginning modern architects and artists as designers. Though Schmidt started under the influence of the English Arts and Crafts (he had traveled in England as a journeyman), his main interest soon became inexpensiveness and production by machinery. As early as 1899–1900 the *Deutsche Werkstätten,* in an exhibition of industrial art in Dresden, showed an apartment of two living-rooms, bedroom, and kitchen for a mere $120. And in 1906, for another exhibition, again in Dresden, they produced their first machine-made furniture, designed by some of the best German architects, such as Bruno Paul. In their catalog of the same year they prided themselves on "developing the style of furniture from the spirit of the machine." This was a feat far more revolutionary than it seems to us today. At that time there were hardly any instances outside Germany of outstanding artists or architects working not for decorative art, but for industrial design, with the exception perhaps of printing in England which just then took the step from the seclusion of such a private venture as the Doves Press into the market for the common man. The important date is 1912, the year of the introduction, thanks to J. H. Mason, of the Imprint type into the fonts of the Monotype Corporation. The *Deutsche Werkstätten* soon went one step further and tackled the problem of standardization of parts. Their first "Unit" furniture, to call it by the name which has become usual in England, was shown in 1910 as *Typenmöbel*. The idea came from America, where it had been in use for some time for bookcases.[83]

The most important step towards the establishment of a universally recognized style out of individual experiments was the foundation of the *Deutscher Werkbund*. In 1907, Muthesius, then Superintendent of the Prussian Board of Trade for Schools of Arts and Crafts, had delivered a public lecture in which, in a very outspoken manner, he warned German crafts and industries against continuing with the imitation of the hackneyed forms of bygone times. The speech roused a storm of indignation with the trades' associations. Discussions became more and more excited and, before the end of the year 1907, a number of adventurous manufacturers together with some architects, artists, and writers, had made up their minds to found a new association, called *Werkbund*, with the aim of "selecting the best representatives of art, industry, crafts and trades, of combining all efforts towards high quality in industrial work, and of forming a rallying-point for all those who are able and willing to work for high quality."[84] *Qualität*, the central idea of the group, was defined as meaning "not only excellent durable work and the use of flawless, genuine materials, but also the attainment of an organic whole rendered *sachlich*, noble, and, if you will, artistic by such means."[85] This definition shows clearly that the *Werkbund* was, from the outset, not opposed to machine production in any respect. In the Inaugural Address at the first Annual Meeting, the architect Theodor Fischer said: "There is no fixed boundary line between tool and machine. Work of a high standard can be created with tools or with machines as soon as man has mastered the machine and made it a tool. . . . It is not the machines in themselves that make work inferior, but our inability to use them properly." And equally it is "not mass production and subdivision of labor that is fatal, but the fact that industry has lost sight of its aim of producing work of the highest quality and does not feel itself to be a serving member of our community but the ruler of the age."[86]

When, in 1915, the Design and Industries Association was founded in England, avowedly inspired by the example of the *Deutscher Werkbund*, it declared in one of its first publications that it was "accepting the machine in its proper place, as a device to be guided and controlled, not merely boycotted."[87] England, with the foundation of the D.I.A., was not early in taking up the program developed by the *Werkbund*. Other Continental countries had followed Germany before the war: the Austrian *Werkbund* dates from 1910, the Swiss from 1913; and the Swedish *Slöjdsförening* was gradually reshaped into a *Werkbund* between 1910 and 1917.

In Germany itself, the existence of this enterprising and uncompromising body did a very great deal to spread the ideals of the Modern Movement. But the *Werkbund* was not the only center. Surprisingly quickly, German art schools had deserted the routine of the nineteenth century and adopted the new course. New principals and new teachers were appointed everywhere. In Prussia, Muthesius was responsible for this. He called Peter Behrens to Düsseldorf and Poelzig to Breslau, both as heads of the existing Academies of Art. Even before that time, Josef Hoffmann had become Professor of Architecture in the Viennese School of Arts and Crafts, and van de Velde head of the Weimar Art School. In 1907, the Berlin School of Arts and Crafts also secured a progressive principal in the person of Bruno Paul.[88]

However, progressive as the spirit in these schools and the *Werkbund* was, the most essential problem was still unsettled, the very problem with which this chapter is mainly concerned. Though machine art was now accepted as one means of artistic expression besides handicraft, where should the stress lie in the future? This problem was for the first time clearly put and explicitly discussed at the Annual Meeting of the *Werkbund* in Cologne in 1914. Muthesius stood up for standardization (*Typisierung*), van de Velde for individualism. Muthesius said: "Architecture and the entire sphere of activity of the *Werkbund* tend towards standardization. It is only by standardization that they can recover that universal importance which they possessed in ages of harmonious civilization. Only by standardization . . . as a salutary concentration of forces, can a generally accepted and reliable taste be introduced." Van de Velde responded: "As long as there are artists in the *Werkbund* . . . they will protest against any proposed canon and any standardization. The artist is essentially and intimately a passionate individualist, a spontaneous creator. Never will he, of his own free will, submit to a discipline forcing upon him a norm, a canon."[89]

But the buildings in the same Cologne Exhibition, above all Gropius' model factory, proved impressively that the future belonged to Muthesius' and not to van de Velde's ideas. Besides, which would a Gothic builder or a Greek sculptor have chosen, individual freedom or the canon? Van de Velde himself has changed his views in the meantime, as he told the author, and, in fact, he said in his speech in 1914 that after some generations the physiognomy of the new style might become sufficiently defined to make standardization feasible. The development has gone faster than van de Velde foresaw. Today, the new style — international, though as clearly divided into national modes as was Romanesque or Gothic art — flourishes in all the artistically creative countries of Western civilization.

It is the chief aim of the following chapters to point out that this new style, the genuine and legitimate style of our century, was achieved by 1914. Morris had started the movement by reviving handicraft as an art worthy of the best men's efforts, the pioneers about 1900 had gone farther by discovering the immense, untried possibilities of machine art. The synthesis, in creation as well as in theory, is the work of Walter Gropius (born in 1883). In 1909, Gropius worked out a memorandum on standardization and mass production of small houses, and on advisable ways of financing such building schemes.[90] At the end of 1914, he began preparing his plans for the reorganization of the Weimar Art School, to which he had been elected principal by the Grand Duke of Saxe-Weimar.[91] The opening of the new school, combining an academy of art and a school of arts and crafts, took place in 1919. Its name was *Staatliches Bauhaus,* and it was to become, for more than a decade, a paramount center of creative energy in Europe. It was at the same time a laboratory for handicraft and for standardization; a school and a workshop. It comprised, in an admirable community spirit, architects, master craftsmen, abstract painters, all working for a new spirit in building. Building to Gropius is a term of wide import. All art, as long as it is sound and healthy, serves building.[92] Hence all students of the Bauhaus were trained as apprentices, received at the end of their course the freedom of the trade, and were only after that admitted to the building-plot and the studio of experimental design.[93]

Gropius regards himself as a follower of Ruskin and Morris, of van de Velde and of the *Werkbund*.[94] So our circle is complete. The history of artistic theory between 1890 and the First World War proves the assertion on which the present work is based, namely that the phase between Morris and Gropius is an historical unit. Morris laid the foundation of the modern style; with Gropius its character was ultimately determined. Art historians speak of "Transitional" preceding the harmonious perfection of "Early Gothic." While Romanesque architecture was still lingering on all over England, William of Sens and the masters of Wells and Lincoln created their immortal works as pioneers of the style to come. What they did for England late in the twelfth century was done at the beginning of this century by Morris and his followers — Voysey, van de Velde, Mackintosh, Wright, Loos, Behrens, Gropius and the other architects and artists — in recognition of whose work the following pages are written.

2

From Eighteen-fifty-one to Morris and the Arts and Crafts

A stodgy and complacent optimism was the frame of mind prevailing in England about 1850. Here was England, thanks to the enterprise of manufacturers and merchants, wealthier than ever, the workshop of the world and the paradise of a successful bourgeoisie, governed by a bourgeois queen and an efficient prince consort. Charity, churchgoing, and demonstrative morality might serve to settle your accounts with Heaven and your conscience — on the whole you were lucky to live in this most progressive and practical age.

No generation before this could have conceived the idea of exhibitions of raw materials and technical products from nations all over the world. The scheme was largely due to Prince Albert's energy. In mapping it out and arranging it, he was carried on the same wave of expansive optimism as his contemporaries.

"Nobody who has paid any attention to the particular features of the present era," said Albert in one of the preparatory addresses, "will doubt for a moment that we are living in a period of most wonderful transition, which tends rapidly to the accomplishment of that great end to which indeed all history points, the realization of the unity of mankind." In the same speech he extolled "the great principle of division of labor, which may be called the moving power of civilization,"[1] and the introduction to the Official Catalogue of the Exhibition asserts that "an event like this exhibition could not have taken place at any other period, and perhaps not among any other people than ourselves." Indeed not; those who wrote these lines knew the reasons and spoke quite frankly about them: "the perfect security for property" and "commercial freedom."[2] The thousands of visitors who thronged the Exhibition probably felt the same. The attendance as well as the size of the buildings and the quantity of products shown was colossal. The esthetic quality of the products was abominable. Sensible visitors realized that, and soon discussions started in England and other countries as to the reasons for such an evident failure. It is easy for us, today, to enumerate various such reasons; but it was hard indeed for a generation that had grown up amid unprecedented discoveries in science and technique. There were the new railways and power-looms, there were the most cunning inventions to facilitate the production of almost any object, formerly made so laboriously by craftsmen — why should these wonderful improvements not help to improve art as well?

Yet this is what resulted: Pardoe, Hoomans & Pardoe's patent velvet pile tapestry carpeting (pl. 1), wrong from any conceivable point of view. You see an extremely elaborate pattern, the charm of which, during the Rococo period, would have been based on the craftsman's imagination and unfailing skill. It is now done by machine, and it looks it. Eighteenth-century ornament may have influenced the designer, the coarseness and overcrowding are his original addition. Moreover he has neglected all fundamental requirements of decoration in general and of carpet decoration especially; we are forced to step over bulging scrolls and into large, unpleasantly realistic flowers; it seems unbelievable that the teachings of Persian carpets should have been so completely forgotten. And this barbarism was by no means limited to England. The other nations exhibiting were equally rich in atrocities. Take the design for a silk shawl by E. Hartneck, shown in the French section (pl. 2). This is at least as incongruous as the English carpet in its mixture of stylization and realism. It shows the same ignorance of that basic need in creating patterns, the integrity of the surface, and the same vulgarity in detail. It was not only that the machine had stamped out taste in industrial products; by 1850 it seemed that it had irremediably poisoned the surviving craftsmen. This is what makes us feel particularly indignant about silverware such as the handmade decanters, goblets, and jugs in plate 3. Why could no craftsman during the eighteenth century produce anything so bulging, so overdone? Surely this contrast is real and not simply a figment of our generation. The insensibility of the artist towards the beauty of pure shape, pure material, pure decorative pattern, is monstrous.

Once more the question has to be asked: Why was this bound to come? The usual answer — because of industrial growth and the invention of machines — is correct, but as a rule taken too superficially. The potter's wheel is a machine, and so are the hand-loom and the printer's press. The development from such simple mechanical devices to modern wonders of machinery was logical and gradual. Why did the machine in the end become so disastrous to art? The transition from the medieval to the modern state of applied art was reached somewhere about the end of the eighteenth century. After 1760, a sudden

1. Carpet from the Great Exhibition of 1851

2. Shawl from the Great Exhibition of 1851

acceleration in technical improvements set in. This no doubt was due to that profound change of mind which began with the Reformation, gathered strength during the seventeenth century, and was dominant in the eighteenth. Rationalism, inductive philosophy, experimental science were the determining fields of European activity during the Age of Reason. Even the religious revival which took place has a strong element of rationalism and marked understanding for worldly tasks and the ethical qualities of workaday life.

The change in European thought was accompanied and followed by a change in social ideals. Thus the newly roused inventiveness received an equally new practical scope. Applied science as a means of governing the world soon became part of a program directed against those classes which had governed during the Middle Ages. Industry meant the bourgeoisie as opposed to the Church and the Nobility. The French Revolution accomplished what had been slowly preparing for more than two centuries. The medieval social system was swept out of existence, and with it the class of cultured and leisurely patrons as well as the class of cultured and guild-trained craftsmen. It is more than coincidence that very soon after the dissolution of the guilds in France (1791), the *Ecole Polytechnique* and the *Conservatoire des Arts et des Métiers* were founded (1795 and 1798), and the first National Industrial Exhibition was held (1798). Industry instead of handicraft is a conception of the *Tiers Etat*. This applies likewise to England; but, owing to the temperament of the English, the change was slower here and came about without a sudden revolution. It started early in the eighteenth century and ended only with the Reform Bill in 1832. Guilds had never been so influential in England as on the Continent. From the sixteenth century on, the nobility had already begun to merge with the merchant class. Plutocracy began to replace aristocracy earlier in England than in France. It is only in a figurative sense that the history of English civilization between 1760 and 1830 can be called the Industrial Revolution.

Some dates may illustrate the rapid and impetuous industrial growth which formed a world capable, a century later, of creating the Modern Movement. As England was leading in the Industrial Revolution nearly all these early dates are English. In 1713, Abraham Darby made cast iron with coke (instead of wood); about 1740 Benjamin Huntsman invented the crucible process of melting steel; in 1783 Cort introduced the puddling process; about 1810 the decisive improvements in the use of the blast-furnace took place (Aubertôt); in 1839 Nasmyth invented the steam hammer; and in 1856 Bessemer his new method of producing steel free from carbon. To these innovations in metallurgy, we must add the invention of the steam engine with separate condenser (J. Watt, 1765), of the steam boiler (1781), the screw steamer (1821), and the railway engine (1825). The princi-

3. Silverware from the Great Exhibition of 1851

23

pal dates in the spinning and weaving industries are the following: 1733 fly-shuttle (J. Kay), 1760 shuttle drop box (R. Kay), 1764–67 spinning jenny (Hargreaves), 1769–75 water-frame for spinning (Arkwright), 1774–79 spinning mule (Crompton), 1785 power-loom (Cartwright), 1799 Jacquard loom.

The immediate consequence of this precipitous development was a sudden increase in production, demanding more and more hands, and so leading to an equally fast increase in population. Towns grew up with horrifying rapidity, new markets had to be satisfied, an ever bigger production was demanded, and inventiveness was stimulated anew. A few more figures may illustrate this rank growth which made our modern world out of a world less similar to ours than to that of the thirteenth and fourteenth centuries. The production of iron in England amounted to about 17,000 tons in 1740, 68,000 in 1788, 170,000 in 1802, 678,000 in 1830. The production of coal in 1810 was 6,000,000 tons, in 1830 25,000,000, in 1857 115,000,000. The export of cotton in 1701 was valued at £23,500, in 1764 at £200,-000, in 1790 at £1,500,000, in 1833 at £18,000,000, in 1840 at £26,500,000. The English population grew before 1750 by about 3% per decade, between 1751 and 1781 by 6% per decade, 1781–91 9%, 1791–1801 11%, 1801–11 14%, 1811–21 18%. Manchester had 8000 inhabitants in 1720, 41,000 in 1744, 102,000 in 1801, 353,000 in 1841; Birmingham, 5000 in 1700, 73,000 in 1801, 183,000 in 1841.

In the midst of this breathless race, no time was left to refine all those innumerable innovations which swamped producer and consumer. With the extinction of the medieval craftsman, the shape and appearance of all products were left to the uneducated manufacturer. Designers of some standing had not penetrated into industry, artists kept aloof, and the workman had no say in artistic matters. Work was bleaker than ever before in European history. Working hours were between twelve and fourteen, doors and windows in factories were kept locked. Children were employed from their fifth or sixth year on. Their hours of work were reduced in 1802, after long struggles, to twelve hours a day. In 1833, 61,000 men, 65,000 women, and 84,000 children under eighteen years of age worked in cotton mills. In mines, no inquiries into accidents were held before 1814.

Economists and philosophers were blind enough to provide an ideological foundation for the criminal attitude of the employer. Philosophy taught that unthwarted development of everybody's energy was the only natural and healthy way of progress.[3] Liberalism ruled unchecked in philosophy as in industry, and implied complete freedom for the manufacturer to produce anything shoddy and hideous, if he could get away with it. And he easily could, because the consumer had no tradition, no education, and no leisure, and was, like the producer, a victim of this vicious circle.

All these facts and considerations have to be taken into account if we are to understand the exhibits of 1851. Contemporary experts failed to do so. They tried changes in the organization of art and especially in art education, but they did not venture to touch the one essential problem, the indissoluble unity of the art of an age and its social system. William Morris alone saw this. Although his solution shirked the problem of machine art, his revival of handicraft would not have been possible, had he not been a social reformer as well as a craftsman. While he followed his inborn passion for making things with his own hands, he

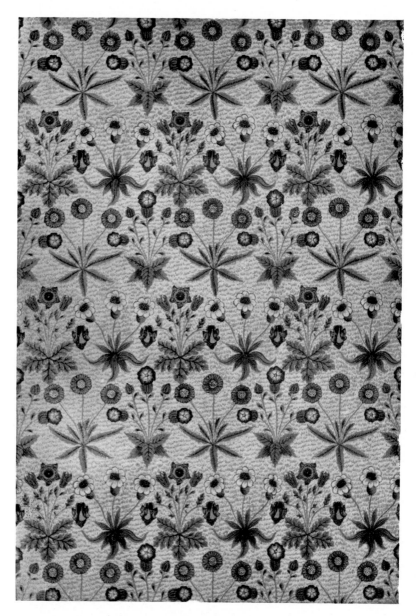

4. Morris: The *Daisy* wallpaper. 1861

knew also that to do this instead of painting pictures was his social duty. Before he was twenty-two, he had experimented with carving in stone and wood, molding in clay, and illuminating. This helped him to acquire a respect for the nature of materials and working processes. Wherever he looked in contemporary industrial art, he saw manufacturers blatantly violating this. So his first furniture for his own rooms was nothing but a protest. The chairs and tables, "intensely medieval, like incubi and succubi" (Rossetti), tell of a deliberate return to the most primitive attitude in shaping domestic objects.

25

At that time, and also in the years when the Red House was furnished and the firm founded, Morris' mode of expression was still somewhat different from that of his later, more famous and more established years. He was still seeking to find the adequate expression for any given task. This is what makes his earliest wallpapers so strikingly fresh and "modern." In the *Daisy,* the second of any he designed, 1861 (pl. 4), the colors are light though restrained, the pattern is pleasantly balanced, without recession, and wholly ornamental without ever losing that intense feeling for nature which is so characteristic of Morris and so different from the imitation of nature as the designers of 1851 practiced it.

Later on, Morris' style becomes broader and statelier and thereby loses some of its youthful and adventurous charm. Not that his creative vein was less abundant now. His very simplicity of approach led him to forms more traditional. When for example, in 1878, he decided to make carpets, he saw that certain oriental patterns were almost exactly what he wanted. Hence his Hammersmith carpets (below) are very much like oriental designs, though he emphasized that he wanted them "obviously to be the outcome of modern and Western ideas."[4] This is remarkable. Morris was so far from inventing decorative forms for invention's sake that, if he found models however remote in space or time which met his purpose, he made use of them or at least came under their spell, even if this happened against his own will.

Herein lies the explanation of the dependence of most of Morris' later chintzes and wallpapers on Gothic models. We are inclined today to overrate the importance of this. Modern writers and artists like to let Morris' design appear all Victorian dullness and gloom and "historicism." That is unjust and deceptive. It is sufficient to compare one of his most famous chintzes, the *Honeysuckle* of 1883 (pl. 6), with a specimen of pre-Morris design

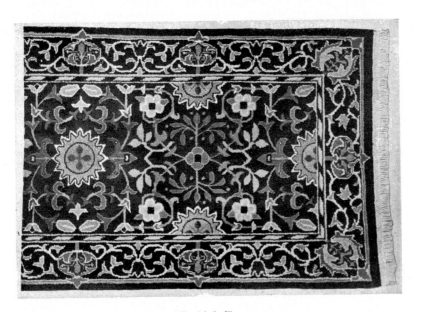

5. Morris: Hammersmith carpet. *The Little Tree* pattern

6. Morris: The *Honeysuckle* chintz. 1883

in textiles such as the shawl from the Great Exhibition (pl. 2), in order to recognize at once the basic contrast between the two. It is not only the contrast between inspiration and imitation; between valuable imitation inspired by fifteenth-century delicacy, and bad imitation vulgarizing eighteenth-century license; it is more. Morris' design is clear and sober, the shawl of 1851 is a messy entwinement of motifs. Its thoughtless concoction of stylization and realism is opposed to Morris' logical unity of composition and close study of

7. Dresser: Cruet sets in silver. 1877–78

growth in nature. The designer of the shawl neglects the decorative law of the coherence of surfaces, while Morris is truly medieval in the spreading out of a flat pattern.

We get exactly the same result if we place Morris' carpet side by side with the carpet of the Exhibition. Again we find live understanding of decorative requirements as opposed to utter neglect of them, and again simplicity and economy as opposed to wasteful confusion. And although it must certainly be admitted that, in stained glass designed by Morris' firm, there is more detail-realism than we can now approve of for ornamental purposes, it must not be forgotten that when Morris began, stained-glass windows were just illustrations with plenty of figures, buildings, and spatial recession, and with a large quantity of colors and shades. His is the merit of having gone back to simple figures, simple attitudes, simple colors, ornamental backgrounds. His Pre-Raphaelite friends and masters helped him in that. Their style in painting differed in the same way from mid-Victorian genre-painting as his from the style of 1851. And if Morris windows do not go further in decorative economy, that is less due to Morris than to Burne-Jones, who could not help remaining a painter, whereas Morris wanted him to be nothing but a decorator.[5]

The revival of decorative honesty in Morris' designs counts for more in the history of the Modern Movement than their connection with bygone styles. Morris the artist may in the end not have been able to reach beyond the limitations of his century, Morris the man and thinker did. This is the reason why his writings and lectures had to be discussed in this book before his artistic achievements.

The first effect of Morris' teaching was that several young artists, architects, and amateurs decided to devote their lives to the crafts. What had been an inferior occupation for more than half a century, became once more a recognized task. There is no need to enumerate them all. Crane and Ashbee have already been mentioned. De Morgan was the great English potter of his age; in glass Powell was foremost; in metal-work Benson; in the arts of the book, Emery Walker and Cobden-Sanderson, the founders of the Doves Press. It is extremely significant that between 1880 and 1890 five societies for the promotion of artistic craftsmanship were started: in 1882 Arthur H. Mackmurdo's Century Guild (the term "Guild" should be noticed), in 1884 the Art Workers' Guild, in the same year the Home Arts and Industries Association, particularly interested in rural crafts, in 1888 Ashbee's Guild and School of Handicraft, and also in 1888 the Arts and Crafts Exhibition Society.

Most of the members of these guilds and associations were a generation younger than Morris, but not all. De Morgan, for instance, was born in 1839, L. F. Day in 1845, Arthur H. Mackmurdo in 1851 (he died in 1942). The work of these artists, if re-examined today, has remarkable surprises in store. Take for instance two cruet sets (pl. 7), produced in 1877 and 1878 by Hukin & Heath's of Birmingham to the designs of Christopher Dresser (1834–1904).[6] Dresser, like Lewis Day, was a professional designer for industrial production. He lectured at South Kensington, traveled in Japan and brought much Eastern art back to his London home. He also designed for Clutha glass and Linthorpe ware (pottery)[7] and wrote several books on the principles of design, sensible but not especially original. This makes the two works illustrated all the more astonishing. In comparison with the silver of the 1851 Exhibition, and actually with most designs for silver and plate done before 1900 or 1905, Dresser's simplicity and creative daring are likewise significant.

8. De Morgan: Plate. 1880's. Victoria and Albert Museum, London

These cruet sets are in every detail reduced to fundamentals, as were Morris' own early designs. The base in one case consists of six plain egg-shaped holders, in the other of an equally plain slab with a low railing. Lids and stoppers are unadorned, and there are hardly any moldings, all the bars being square or round.

Again if we look at a plate with a gazelle (pl. 8), made by De Morgan at his Merton Works between 1882 and 1888 and now at the Victoria and Albert Museum in London, the same understanding of decorative fundamentals appears, only this time in terms of two instead of three dimensions. There is of course dependence on Persia, but the bold and ornamental draftsmanship of the tree behind the sharply outlined animal, and the symbol of water behind the fishes are remarkably original.

However, nothing in the eighties was as daringly personal as some of Mackmurdo's designs.[8] His title page to a book (below), which he had written himself in defense of Sir Christopher Wren's London City churches, just then in danger of wholesale destruction, has as its chief motif a completely asymmetrical feathery leaf ornament of a kind never seen in Morris or Crane or any of the other representatives of the Arts and Crafts. Its immense importance for the development of ornament in the nineties will come out in a later chapter.

Meanwhile it should not be forgotten that such directness of approach was still very exceptional. Most of the craftsmen who followed Morris remained faithful to his standards, faithful, too, in refusing any drastic breach with tradition. In this no doubt they proved English above all. It seems very understandable that England led the growing Modern Movement exactly as long as it did not mean a complete break with traditions. This applies to architecture just as much as to design, and so we find England between 1860 and 1900 as the leading European country in both.

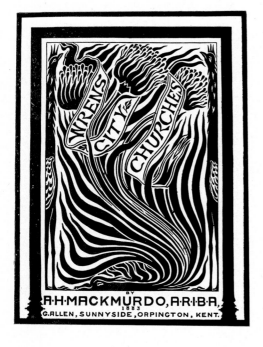

9. Mackmurdo: Title page. 1883

10. Webb: The Red House, Bexley Heath, Kent. Built in 1859 for William Morris

All through the development of architecture in the principal European countries from 1850 to the end of the century, the same direction can be noticed. The high tide of the Gothic Revival (Houses of Parliament: Barry and Pugin, 1835–52) was passing about 1865, though later and yet pure Neo-Gothic buildings are of course to be found in many places (Town Hall, Manchester: Waterhouse, 1868–77; Glasgow University: G. G. Scott, 1870; Natural History Museum, London: Waterhouse, 1873–80). Simple Neo-Renaissance was also coming to an end (Reform Club: Barry, designed 1837; Dresden Opera: Semper, first building 1838–41; Dresden Gallery: Semper, 1847–54). The next phase was the revival everywhere of an overdecorated type of Nordic Renaissance (in Paris the *Hôtel de Ville,* already begun in 1837, in England Neo-Elizabethan, in Germany *Neudeutsche* Renaissance, after 1870). Immediately after the introduction of this style of decoration, an equally overdecorated but more colossal Neo-Baroque set in (Paris *Opéra:* Garnier, 1861–74; Brussels *Palais de Justice:* Poelaert, 1866–83). This style remained the official architectural taste in most Continental countries until after 1900.

In England the evolution followed precisely the same course; but, since English architecture had been so different from Continental during the centuries imitated, the result was likewise different. The background in England was something like this. The overcrowded Elizabethan and Jacobean Mannerism was superseded in the seventeenth century by Inigo Jones's and then by Christopher Wren's stately and dignified classicism, and this grand yet reserved style remained dominant throughout the eighteenth century as far as churches and large houses were concerned. It was otherwise with domestic architecture of a more intimate character. In this, since the Middle Ages, England had developed an unobtrusive, dignified,

31

11. Webb: No. 1 Palace Gardens, Kensington, London. 1868

and comfortable style of her own. After the accession of William of Orange, even royal palaces (Kensington Palace) began to exhibit these qualities. They are the keynote in the style of London's squares and streets; they give London her distinctive character.

In 1859, Morris asked Philip Webb (1831–1915), his friend and colleague in Street's studio, to design a house for him and his wife. It was built in a spirit contrary to that of the past century. As in his decorative designs, Morris refused any connection with Italy and the Baroque and aimed at something akin to the style of the late Middle Ages. Webb applied certain Gothic details such as pointed arches and high-pitched roofs; he also adopted the irregularity of the fourteenth and fifteenth-century domestic and especially monastic architecture, but he never copied. He even admitted the sash windows of William and Mary and Queen Anne without ever being afraid of clashes between the various styles to which he went for inspiration. The Red House as a whole is a building of a surprisingly independent character, solid and spacious looking and yet not in the least pretentious (pl. 10). This is

32

12. Shaw: New Zealand Chambers, Leadenhall St., London. 1872–73

perhaps its most important feature. The architect does not imitate palaces. In designing he thinks of a wealthy middle class. He shows the red brick of the façades without covering it with plaster as Neo-Classic rules prescribed, and takes the outside appearance of the house as an expression of inside requirements without attempting a grand and useless symmetry.

In town architecture the counterpart of the Red House is the house at No. 1 Palace Gardens in Kensington, London, which Webb designed in 1868 (pl. 11). It exhibits fearlessly two Queen Anne windows and between them a brick pier of obvious Gothic derivation supporting an oriel window on a curious ribbed cove. Of the Domestic Revival, as the movement in English town and country architecture between 1860 and 1900 is often called, Webb remained the strongest and soundest, if not the most brilliant exponent. If one looks for brilliance, fecundity of invention and sheer joy in novelty, one has to go to Richard Norman Shaw (1831–1912)[9] and not to Webb. Shaw's large country houses (or rather the country houses of the Shaw–Eden Nesfield partnership) start in a theatrical, undisciplined,

13. Shaw: The architect's house, Ellerdale Road, Hampstead, London. 1875

14. Shaw: No. 170 Queen's Gate, London. 1888

34

15. Nesfield: Kinmel Park, Abergele, Wales. 1866

flamboyant imitation-Tudor, still entirely pre-Morris in spirit. The most characteristic examples are Leys Wood in Sussex, 1869, and Grims Dyke near London, 1872. Then, immediately after Grims Dyke, Shaw changed to something much more original. The seventeenth century caught his fancy, and in his first city building, the New Zealand Chambers in Leadenhall Street, London (pl. 12), now unfortunately bombed out, he dared to combine bay windows of a lively English provincial appearance on the second and third floors with a ground floor exhibiting hardly anything but two large office windows of many panes separated by wooden glazing bars. That was in 1872–73. In 1875 his own house in Ellerdale Road, Hampstead, London, is of equal boldness (pl. 13). The key motifs now comprise, besides Dutch curved gables of the shape popular in England between 1630 and 1660, the tall slim sash windows of William and Mary and Queen Anne architecture. The composition is deliberately picturesque, but very sensitively balanced and by no means haphazard.

However successful this so-called Queen Anne Revival was, Norman Shaw did not in the long run remain satisfied with it. There was yet another change in his style — or rather the source of his style; for he remained to the end faithful to historicism as such, even if his was a very cavalier treatment of historical precedent. It was in the late eighties that he remembered what his former partner Eden Nesfield (1835–88) had done as far back as 1866 (above) and studied in earnest the style of the smaller country and town house of the later seventeenth and early eighteenth centuries in England, not only for window motifs but for the whole of their plain, sensible, well-proportioned, unadorned brick frontages. Nesfield's Kinmel Park stands, as far as we can see, quite on its own; Shaw's house at No. 170 Queen's Gate, London of 1888 (pl. 14) started a fashion which reached its climax only in the twentieth century. It comes indeed as near to the spirit of the new century as one could come without actually breaking with the past, and in this respect it was more pro-

35

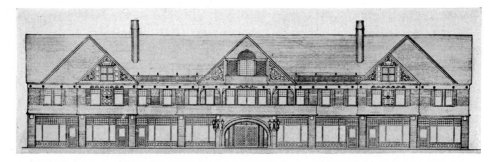

16. White: Newport Casino. 1881

17. White: Germantown Cricket Club, Philadelphia. 1891

gressive than the work of any of Shaw's contemporaries at home and abroad.

Yet England was not entirely alone in its domestic innovations. There was one other country which showed as much and occasionally even more esthetic enterprise, the United States. It was the first time in its architectural history that America appeared in the vanguard. The architect who advanced so boldly was Henry Hobson Richardson (1838–86).[10] His F. L. Ames gate lodge in North Easton, Mass., 1880–81, and his Stoughton house in Cambridge, Mass., of 1882–83 (pl. 18) are even less derivative than Shaw's contemporary houses. Richardson's use of shingling and of large-scale random rubble, of boulders, one is tempted to say, and of picturesque asymmetry shows as much originality as Shaw possessed and more vigor. His even more impressive power in the designing of commercial structures will be mentioned later. Both his town and his country styles were at once widely imitated by good, bad and indifferent architects. Amongst his best followers was Stanford White (1853–1906) whose Newport Casino was built as early as 1881 (pl. 16). The same quali-

18. Richardson: Stoughton house, Cambridge, Massachusetts. 1882–83

ties are here clearly visible as in the Stoughton house though perhaps handled a little more elegantly.

Stanford White, less elementary and less hard than Richardson, could indeed take the same step which Shaw had taken between the houses of 1875 and of 1888. Only in the case of White the new ideal of simplicity was not expressed in terms of English Queen Anne but first in terms of the Central Italian High Renaissance and then of American Colonial. The examples are well enough known: The Villard house on Madison Avenue, New York, of 1885 and the H. A. C. Taylor house in Newport, R.I., of 1886 or the Germantown Cricket Club, Philadelphia, of 1891[11] (pl. 17).

However stimulating and original these American developments were, they did not have any immediate repercussions on architecture in Europe. In England occasional similarities with Richardson occur (and will be referred to in a later chapter), but the Continent remained unaware of American innovations for a surprisingly long time. When Continental architects had grown weary of the boastful spirit of Neo-Baroque, and had freed themselves from all period forms by a short plunge into *Art Nouveau,* they looked to England for help, to English building and English crafts, and not yet to America.

3

Eighteen-ninety in Painting

Whereas the way for a future style in architecture and design was cleared by English artists, the new ideals in painting were conceived and developed on the Continent. The part played by England in the growing movement was to maintain and revive wholesome traditions in order to secure a solid foundation upon which the structure could be built; the task which Continental artists had set themselves was to force a new faith upon the world of art.

Morris had declined to follow the ways of the generation preceding him; the leading Continental artists with whom we shall have to deal in this chapter did the same, or, as it would be better to say, outwardly the same. For Morris turned against the horrors of 1851, the reformers of 1890 against Manet, Renoir, and the other Impressionists, artists of brilliant skill. Morris loathed the superficiality of his immediate predecessors and that Liberalism which was responsible for the social and artistic conditions in England; the rebels of 1890 also accused their predecessors of superficiality (though in the changed sense of exclusive regard for surface qualities) and of more concern with personal than with community interests, which is the philosophical corollary of Liberalism.

That far, the Morris Movement and the movement in painting which took shape about 1890 advanced on comparable lines and towards comparable aims. But there is one chief difference of means and ends. Morris dreamed of a revival of medieval society, medieval craft, and medieval forms; the leaders of European painting in 1890 fought for something that had never existed before. On the whole, their style was free from period revival, unencumbered and uncompromising. This would also apply to the architecture and decoration of *Art Nouveau;* but the break was achieved by the painters earlier than by the architects. Therefore an account of the revolution in painting has to be given before we can continue the discussion of architectural and decorative evolution, which is the main task of the present work.

Many artists took part in this destructive and constructive movement. The most powerful characters were two Frenchmen, Cézanne and Gauguin, a Dutchman, van Gogh, and a Norwegian, Munch. Five more, besides these, shall be mentioned here: Seurat, Rousseau, Ensor, Toorop, Hodler.

A comparison between a *Bathers,* c. 1897 by Renoir (pl. 19) and one by Cézanne 1895–1905 (pl. 20), may serve to illustrate the violent change which characterizes European painting about 1890. Cézanne (1839–1906), though born during the same decade as Manet, Renoir, and Monet, was an Impressionist only for a short time. His early style was derived

19. Renoir: Bathers. c.1897. Barnes Foundation, Merion, Pennsylvania

20. Cézanne: Bathers. 1895–1905. The Philadelphia Museum of Art

from Delacroix, Courbet, and the Baroque, and while even in his most mature works he keeps that beauty of the surface which was the sole ideal of Impressionism, his own ideal was in other ways wholly opposed to theirs. The surface of a landscape by Monet is a glittering veil, Cézanne's hills and trees and houses are still and monumental planes, reposing in the three-dimensional space of the picture.

The charm of Renoir's *Bathers* lies in the play of rosy young bodies, in a landscape of loosely sketched-in green and bluish and pinkish tones. It is a highly sensuous charm. Renoir said frankly that in front of a masterpiece he thought of only one thing: to enjoy it. He once praised a picture by saying that he wanted to kiss it, and he blamed a great painter because "he had never caressed the canvas."[1] To catch all the bliss of a passing instant, all the joy in what the eye can drink in of light and color any day and any moment, to make a round, harmonious composition of it and to paint it with all its atmospheric glamor: that is Renoir's aim.

Cézanne despised such a superficial approach. The women in his *Bathers* are without any sensuous appeal. They act not on their own but on behalf of an abstract scheme of construction which is the real subject of the picture. His aim is to express the lasting qualities of objects; no transitory beauty occupies his mind. The striding woman on the left is a diagonal to be continued in the unnaturally slanting trees. The powerful curve of the back and thigh of the figure sitting on the left serves to join these diagonals with the four main horizontals. The faces are hardly detailed, no personal expression is allowed. Cézanne does not care for the individual, he speculates on the idea of the Universe. "That gang of Impressionists," he once exclaimed, "lack a master as well as an idea."[2] By constructing his pictures with "cylinder, sphere and cone,"[3] Cézanne strove to paraphrase the eternal laws of Nature. Hence he was almost bound to take endless pains over his works, altering and restarting them over and over again. Up to fifty sittings were necessary for a portrait, and many of them evidence this passionate exertion.

For the intensity and passion of Vincent van Gogh (1853–1890), this exertion proved too much. His mind gave way as soon as he had achieved his task. The course of van Gogh's life is extremely significant of the changed attitude which inspired the creative artists about 1890. He went as a lay-preacher to the poor and destitute, before he had found in painting an adequate means of expression, and he had to work hard to acquire the craft of the brush. His mature style is to be found in the works of only two years, pictures that he painted in a frantic hurry, "like the harvester who works silently in the blazing sun, concentrating on his work."[4] A picture may represent an empty chair only, but it means the chair which is empty, now that the friend has tragically departed — and all the overwhelming violence of his feeling is in its colors and the infuriated strokes of broad brushes. He may paint a café, but he paints it as "a place where one can run mad, or commit a crime."[5] His color above all is never accidental, never just the rendering of shades observed in nature. The introduction of a new color always suggests an "emotion of an ardent temperament,"[6] maybe "the thought of a brow," or "the love of two lovers."[7]

So not one of his mature portraits is only a portrait, only the representation of the features of some indifferent person. In a mysterious way, much more is embedded in the lines

21. Manet: Jeanne (Springtime). 1882. The Metropolitan Museum of Art, New York
22. Van Gogh: Portrait. 1890. Collection Mrs. Hedy Hahnloser-Bühler, Winterthur, Switzerland

of such a face, the rude shape of such a body, the hard strokes of such a background (pl. 22). Again we feel of a sudden confronted with Nature as a creative force, magnificent and terrifying, and not with the changing surface of nature as skilfully portrayed by the Impressionist. Manet, in his *Jeanne* (*Springtime*) of 1882 (pl. 21), hardly differentiates between the consistence of the human being and that of the surroundings. This refusal to distinguish between the changing and the lasting, the absolute and the accidental, had emerged in philosophy since the seventeenth century; it created the art of the Dutch landscape, and culminated in Impressionism. Jeanne is of importance to the artist only in so far as she reflects nature, reflects color and light.

But to van Gogh the peasant woman, as he knew her so well, is the vessel of an idea. She is sacred and indestructible as a symbol. He was longing to paint "pictures of saints and holy women from life which would seem to belong to another age, and they would be middle-class women of the present day."[8] He wanted to address the people, and believed that they, in buying cheap and coarse color prints, were on the right path, rather than those city dwellers who went to the art exhibitions.[9] He preferred the simplicity of the popular color print to the refinement of contemporary painting, and strove towards a similar simplicity of subject and technique. Only diffidence and underestimation of his own powers prevented him from venturing upon religious subjects. He actually began to paint a *Garden of Gethsemane,* but destroyed it afterwards. By painting all day long, he hoped to drown this "terrible need of religion."[10] But he failed; the "terrible need" appears in whatever he did,

41

23. Van Gogh: The Starry Night. 1889. The Museum of Modern Art, New York. Acquired through the Lillie P. Bliss Bequest

and lends that convulsive intensity to any man, or flower, or cloud that he chooses as an object for his devotion.

As his life drew to its close, that intensity increased. Compared with what he painted during the last twelve months or so of his life, even his own works painted a year before the first attack of illness seem happy and balanced. Only now in a landscape like the one in the collection of the Museum of Modern Art in New York (above) is there that immediate revelation of a vast creative force moving sun, stars and trees and leaving the puny cottages and the church at the mercy of tempestuous whirlpools infinitely stronger than the stones and timbers patiently stuck together by human hands.

It is true, this cosmic terror was felt so violently by van Gogh alone. But would Gauguin (1848–1903) have left Europe and started a new life amongst the savages of Pacific islands, if he too had not dreaded the shallowness of nineteenth-century life? Before he went, he turned for a short time, no doubt under the influence of van Gogh's missionary zeal, to religious painting. There is, in the Edinburgh Gallery, the strange picture of Jacob wrestling with the Angel, with the foreground of Breton women, and there is the *Yellow Christ,* illustrated in plate 24. An Impressionist painter could never have been satisfied with these

42

24. Gauguin: Yellow Christ. 1889. The Albright Art Gallery, Buffalo, New York

wooden forms, so harsh and unpleasing, and with these heavy, solid, intense colors, nor would an Impressionist have chosen this subject. The Impressionist is interested only in what he can see with his own eyes, and nothing behind the surface is important. He is as materialistic as any Victorian philosopher. To Gauguin the surface is immaterial, the casual arrangement of objects in nature is no more than a stimulus for the conception of a picture. The essential process is to condense from the impression received something which contains all the factors of lasting significance. In the *Yellow Christ* the background is not one particular piece of French scenery, it is a general symbol of France, and of the spirit of peasant life, close to the soil and pious in an elementary, unreasoning way. There is no thought in the faces of these women, none of the anecdotic interest which the Impressionist would

43

25. Gauguin: The Moon and the Earth (*Hina Tefatu*). 1893. The Museum of Modern Art, New York. Lillie P. Bliss Collection

provide. Tiredness after hard work, resignation, and dumb submission are all they express. The Christ in the center of the picture also has all the deliberate primitiveness with which the Expressionists of 1920 endowed their figures — an idol, not an image of Christ cruci-fied, as the five centuries before Gauguin had evolved it.

No wonder that Gauguin abandoned a Europe whose development had led to such petty sophistication and materialism. In the Pacific he found men and women naïve and untouched by the twisted reasoning of Paris, trusting instinct and their passions; he found nature fertile and untrimmed, and a religion in which that nature and the fears and desires of those men and women had taken the shapes of fetishes and apparitions. The picture of *The Moon and the Earth* (above) was painted only four years after the *Yellow Christ,* and the choice of color is indeed still the same. But what had been aggressive and jerky, has now become broad and round and fulfilled. Where in the Breton painting the landscape still formed a background to the scene, the woman, the idol and the well are now one, one in the tapestry-

26. Gauguin: Women at the River (*Auti Te Pape*). c.1891–93. The Museum of Modern Art, New York. Lillie P. Bliss Collection

like surface on the canvas, and one in essence: the woman like a brown tree trunk, the idol like a dark rock. Nature has taken back what Western civilization had wrested from her.

Nature in this sense, that is the spirit of nature versus the imitation of the surface appearance of nature, and also, in a much broader sense, nature as a universal power versus human independence is one of the mottoes of the new movement in European painting about 1890. It may mean, as in Gauguin and van Gogh, back to instinct and self-abandon, or it may mean, as in Cézanne, back to the fundamentals of geometry. It may lead to Expressionism or to Cubism. It may go for inspiration to cylinder, sphere and cone, or to Polynesian and medieval carving; the essential attitude of opposition to the mentality of the nineteenth century remains the same.

One typical outcome of the rediscovery of early art at its most forceful was a change of style in the graphic arts, initiated by Gauguin in his zincographs of 1889. The effect of these prints is confined to violent contrasts of flat surfaces. All delicate shades and atmospheric transitions are abandoned. No wonder that after a few years Gauguin resorted to another even more suitable medium for expressing in black and white those visions which occupied his mind. The woodcut relying entirely on the process of carving with a knife should not seek after effects that are not simple and strong (above). Only by a perverse *tour de force* could nineteenth-century wood engravers produce superficially something like the subtle charm of etchings.

Gauguin's first woodcuts date from 1894. Earlier than this the Swiss painter Félix Vallotton (1865–1925)[11] had discovered the possibilities of the woodcut for expressing the new feelings of 1890. In his woodcuts of 1892 and 1893, *The Anarchist* or *Young Girls,* he goes so far in reducing nuances and stressing a few main features and gestures as to approach caricature. And his principal picture of this period, *The Bath* (pl. 27), is perhaps the most astonishing example of deliberate infantilism that was produced by that generation. In a highly scandalizing manner, Vallotton has combined a few stylized figures in grotesque chemises with ten or twelve obtrusively drawn nudes. No wonder that he became one of the leaders in the conversion of posters into works of art. His posters begin in 1892.

From the same years date the first French posters whose value is based on the opposition of simple and brightly colored surfaces and the abolition of space (Toulouse-Lautrec, Steinlen). English artists, above all the Beggarstaffs (J. Pryde and W. Nicholson), joined this movement almost at once and produced some of the most striking posters (*Cinderella*, Drury Lane Theatre, 1894).[12]

This elementary style, reminiscent of the old broadsheet, is also one of the prominent features in the paintings of Seurat and Rousseau. The *Grande Jatte* (pl. 28) by Georges Seurat (1859–91) appeared as a joke when it was painted in 1886. The figures are wooden like children's toys, they move as awkwardly as if they were driven by clockwork inside, along invisible rails running parallel to the frame of the picture. We seem to hear the *tic-tac* of their movements. The dogs and the ridiculous little monkey have no life either. This deliberate elimination of atmosphere is all the more remarkable, as Seurat had started from Impressionism and had developed his strange mosaic-like technique while endeavoring to push to its extreme the scientific principle which underlies the Impressionist dissolution of the surface. The Impressionists had painted in loose touches and commas of unmixed color so as to leave to the eye of the beholder the task of gathering up the separate dots. This helped to create that effect of blurred atmosphere which, to the convinced Impressionist, equals the world. Seurat, in condensing these flaky spots into small solid units, destroyed the

27. Vallotton: The Bath. 1890. Collection Paul Vallotton, Lausanne, Switzerland

46

28. Seurat: A Sunday Afternoon on the Island of La Grande Jatte. 1884–86. The Art Institute of Chicago (Helen Birch Bartlett Memorial Collection)

effect aimed at by Renoir and Monet and replaced it by an unreal effect of hieratic stiffness.

Seurat must have enjoyed the shock which this apparently childish stiffness gave the public. Otherwise, he would not have painted those circus scenes, like the *Chahut* (1890) and the *Circus Parade* (1888), with the grotesque acrobats and dancers, petrified, it seems, in the most distorted attitudes. Here again, we are confronted with revolt — as much as in Cézanne's *Bathers,* or van Gogh's landscapes, or Gauguin's Tahiti women — a sudden revelation of the futility of modern civilization.

Only one painter among those most characteristic of 1890 had nothing of that feeling: Rousseau, *le douanier* (1844–1910), to whom destiny had given such a child-like mind that he could paint primitively without any conscious revulsion. This art has none of the esthetic subtleties of Manet or Degas. But this loss in esthetic value is counterbalanced by an increase in live value, and that is in our context tantamount to historical value.

In his life-size self portrait of 1890 (pl. 29), the colors are crude as in an old-fashioned calendar illustration, the forms are as if drawn by a child. This pretty array of flags, those prim clouds with the balloon floating about, and the black silhouette of the painter himself looking rather cross, might have appeared the aberration of an untalented amateur. Today we can see that all this corresponds to Seurat's and Vallotton's tendencies, and marks a milestone in the development of Western art.

47

29. Rousseau: Self Portrait. 1890. Modern Gallery, Prague

Like Gauguin, Rousseau felt attracted by the primitive life of the tropics. He had once seen them, and, years later, he began to paint primeval forests, lions, tigers, monkeys, and lion-hunters. It is not easy to appreciate his attitude in doing this. His pictures lack that sacred quality which Gauguin, and later on Nolde, embedded in their simple tales. But they are strikingly sincere in their childish treatment, with trees and wild animals such as infants would enjoy and fear in their picture-books. It may well be that, by such an apparently help-less technique, Rousseau has come nearer to the world of the savages than Gauguin with his superior knowledge of art.

At first sight one may also take the many paintings by James Ensor (1860–) which rep-resent masked revelers as mere fun. But their true meaning is entirely opposed to that of

30. Ensor: Intrigue. 1890. Royal Museum, Antwerp

31. Ensor: Tribulations of St. Anthony. 1887. The Museum of Modern Art, New York. Purchase Fund

Seurat's or Rousseau's works. Ensor too had been an Impressionist for some time. He began to paint masks even before he broke away from the tenets of Impressionism. In his mature works, those painted since about 1886 (pl. 30), there is nothing of Impressionist naturalism, nothing either of Rousseau's simple-heartedness or Seurat's directness of approach. He painted those groups of people with their grinning masks not because he enjoyed festive confusion, but because the mask allows the artist to fix a lasting expression of demoniac villainy to a face. This is again a denial of the nuance, a "back to fundamentals," though to En-

32. Khnopff: Arum Lily. 1895. Whereabouts unknown

sor the ultimate fundamental to be reached is the baseness of human nature. The truth of this interpretation of his attitude can be proved by looking at other subjects which Ensor painted or etched during those decisive years. His principal paintings are the *Tribulations of St. Anthony* of 1887 (pl. 31) and *The Entry of Christ into Brussels* of 1888. Here again the Saint or the God is surrounded by hideous demons made even more terrifying by the softness and sometimes sugariness of Ensor's colors. But where such fleshy pinks and silky blues and sweet rich greens serve to add to the sheer surface joy of an Impressionist painting, they intensify in Ensor the grim contrast with the anxieties of the scenes he depicts.

Wherever one looks, a new conception of the "subject-picture" is an integral part of the movement of 1890. Thinking of Impressionism we think of landscapes, portraits, still lifes, not of religion and philosophy. There were, it is true, many outside Impressionism who painted patriotic or allegorical subjects and anecdote and genre, but amongst the spiritual leaders few between the English Pre-Raphaelites, that is the last descendants of early nineteenth-century Romanticism, and the pioneers of 1890 took an interest in subject matter as such. And when the movement of 1890 turned once more to symbolism, inspiration came more often than is usually realized through the manifold, if not very deep, channels of the English Arts and Crafts which were still fed from the Pre-Raphaelite fountainhead. Such is the case with the two French painters who stood out between 1860 and 1890 as exponents of an art expressive of thoughts more profound than what everyday life could offer: Gustave Moreau (1826–98), Huysman's friend, and Odilon Redon (1840–1916).

33. Toorop: Faith Giving Way. 1891. Municipal Museum, The Hague

The connecting link between Moreau, the Pre-Raphaelites, and the new style of 1890 is the work of the Belgian Fernand Khnopff (1858–1921). His mother and his wife were English, and he himself had spent several years in England. His first symbolistic picture, *Sphinx,* was painted in 1884. His principal works date from about 1891–96 (*The Offering,* 1891). The allegorical portrait shown in plate 32 is called *Arum Lily* (1895). The young figure stands erect, with her arm and hand held stiffly, like a ritual dancer. Her intensely composed face, the face of an archangel, is turned aside. A deliberate parallelism exists between the high and slender growth of the lily and of the young woman.

To the position of Khnopff in Belgium corresponds that of Jan Toorop (1858–1928) in Holland. He too started under the influence of French nineteenth-century tendencies, he too acquired a personal knowledge of England (about 1885) and he too arrived at symbolism about 1890. The cartoon which is called *Faith Giving Way* (above) was drawn in 1891 and

51

34. Hodler: The Chosen One. 1893–94. Kunstmuseum, Berne, Switzerland

is Toorop's first work showing the new style fully developed: an odd entwinement of gaunt limbs, understandable only by reading an elaborate program. Both this obscurity and the intricacy of the pattern of human bodies bear witness to two more sources of Toorop's style, one doubtful, the other certain; namely Blake's linear art and hermetic symbolism, and the arts of Java, brought close to Toorop by Holland's eastern possessions. It is indeed illuminating in this connection to remember that Toorop was born in Java, and that about 1899 Holland began to imitate Indonesian Batik-printing, just as Gauguin in his rare wood carvings imitated the idols of Tahiti.

More successful than Toorop's and purer than Gauguin's was the style of the Swiss Ferdinand Hodler (1853–1918) which was developed to express sacred truth in terms of line and cool precise color. Hodler's first portrait, showing a marked tendency towards hieratic simplification, dates from 1888; his first allegorical picture, *The Night,* from 1890. The painting called *The Chosen One,* which is illustrated above, was conceived in 1893 and carried out in 1893–94. A tapestry, not a picture: that is what we feel. No spatial, and above all no atmospheric values are admitted. The six guardian angels do not stand on the ground; they are supposed to be flying, but do not give any such impression. Neither is there any air between their feet and the grass, or between their bodies and the background. As six long and slender candle-like shapes, they surround in a shallow ellipse the small and sparse figure of the boy praying. His arms and hands are again as delicate as those drawn by Toorop or Khnopff. Sensuous charm of flesh and skin would detract from the main content. An icy air of clear abstraction rests upon Hodler's work. No wonder that, in his old age, he turned towards Alpine landscapes. Artists who struggled for such purity of style and precision of rendering were bound to look down scornfully on the surface realism and loose composition of the Impressionist school.

But the greatest Germanic painter of his generation, much greater in power than Hodler and Toorop, is Edvard Munch (1863–1944). Like so many of the leaders of that generation, he had gone through a phase of Impressionism. But while working in Paris under the influence of Pissarro, he imbibed, first perhaps unconsciously, the style of Gauguin, and thus gained strength to overcome the dangerous charm of superficial beauty. Soon he started, in a surprisingly original manner, simplifying and leaving out all non-essential features. By the beginning of the nineties, the phase of transition was at an end. His paintings, woodcuts, and lithographs of 1893, 1894, 1895 are a synthesis of the new movement's Germanic aspect, as strong and as serious an van Gogh's paintings and drawings of 1889 and 1890, and yet utterly different in appearance.

In the picture *The Cry* (pl. 35), natural data are reduced to the minimum: sea, hill, beach, and pier. More than that would be unnecessary. The face of the shrieking creature — we do not even recognize its sex — is defined only so far as the intense expression demands. The cry shapes this face, and it pervades the whole picture, carried by visible waves of sound. So Munch achieves his symbolical expression of the oneness and the Strind-bergian horror of the Universe. The subject matters as much to him as to Toorop and Hodler. He painted *Jealousy* and *Puberty,* and even such critical subjects as *The Kiss* and *The Day After.* But he is never sophisticated, or verbose, or melodramatic, though during these years of open revolt, he seems at times to work under morbid obsessions.

But the quality, above all, which raises Munch to the level of van Gogh is that he does not depend on the symbolic subject. He is just as strong in his landscapes and portraits. Whatever he paints, he makes us feel the inexhaustible power of Nature parturient.

How far, that is the most essential question in our context, do the new tendencies of the painters discussed here coincide with or bear upon those of the architectural style of the Modern Movement? In summing up the qualities which distinguish the artists of 1890 from their predecessors, an attempt will be made to emphasize those which find an echo in contemporary architecture and decoration.

Instead of a variety of charming surface effects, Cézanne, Gauguin, Rousseau believe in the unbroken flat surface; Hodler, Munch, Toorop in the rhythmically drawn outline, as a more intense means of artistic expression. Strong colors and primitive shapes replace the abundance of delicate nuances; hard schemes of composition, the liberty of apparently casual picturesqueness. Not closeness to reality but expressiveness of pattern is what matters; not quick observation of natural facts but their perfect translation onto a plane of abstract significance. Carried over into the artist's personal outlook, this means seriousness, religious conscience, fervent passion, and no longer spirited play or skilful craftsmanship. It means, instead of art for art's sake, art serving something higher than art itself can be.

Exactly the same qualities appear at the same time in literature. The movement away from naturalism and surface interest in the widest sense of these words was universal. It can be seen in the Belgian Maeterlinck (born in 1862) and his *Pelléas et Mélisande* of 1892, in the Englishman Oscar Wilde's (born 1854) *Salome* of 1893, in the German Hauptmann's

35. Munch: The Cry. 1893. National Gallery, Oslo

(born 1862) sudden change from his *Weavers* of 1892 to his *Hannele* of 1893, and in France even earlier in Verlaine, Mallarmé and Rimbaud (born in 1844, 1842, and 1854 respectively).

But, just as in painting, there are two aspects to this literary movement. Symbolism may be a strength and a weakness — an endeavor towards sanctity or an affectation. Cézanne and van Gogh stand on the one side, Toorop and Khnopff on the other, the former strong, self-disciplined and exacting, the latter weak, self-indulgent and relaxing. So the one led into a future of fulfillment, that is the establishment of the Modern Movement of the twentieth century, the other into the blind alley of *Art Nouveau*. It is with *Art Nouveau* that we must now first concern ourselves.

4

Art Nouveau

If the long, sensitive curve, reminiscent of the lily's stem, an insect's feeler, the filament of a blossom or occasionally a slender flame, the curve undulating, flowing and interplaying with others, sprouting from corners and covering asymmetrically all available surfaces, can be regarded as the *leitmotif* of *Art Nouveau,* then the first work of *Art Nouveau* which can be traced is Arthur H. Mackmurdo's cover of his book on Wren's City Churches published in 1883, and illustrated on page 30 as an example of the English Arts and Crafts. From Mackmurdo and a few other English designers such as, for instance, Heywood Sumner[1] the new message of freedom and originality, of delicate line and perhaps of *fin de siècle* elaboration and *raffinement* went to that brilliant *décadent,* Aubrey Beardsley,[2] who had only eight years to show his questionable genius before he died in 1898 at the age of twenty-six. He had begun as a belated follower of the Pre-Raphaelites, and broken away from them in 1892 while he was working on the illustrations to the *Morte d'Arthur.* In a vignette of his such as *The 'Cello Player* of 1893 (pl. 36), the influence of Rossetti and Burne-Jones is still visible, though the shape of the head is longer, the hands are longer and more nervous, and the contours of the figure together with the slender stalks of the sunflowers form a pattern almost independent of natural data. This fact especially links Beardsley with the ideals of *Art Nouveau.* A particularly complete example of his exceedingly personal and *outré* handwriting is the drawing *Siegfried* (pl. 37), published in 1893 in the first issue of *The Studio.* The arrangement of short C-curves, little flowers, lines of minute dots, is different from the manner of any other artist. The way in which Beardsley covers tree trunks and flower stalks and the body of the monster with dainty ornament, shows how regardless he is of the meaning of the scene represented. His concern is with decoration, a graceful display of ingenious draftsmanship. All this has nothing to do with Siegfried, or with Wagner and only very little with the serious-mindedness of the Pre-Raphaelites, Morris and the Arts and Crafts.[3]

A similarity of approach and graphic style between Beardsley and the Toorop of the same years will be evident to anybody who remembers the *Faith Giving Way* illustrated in the previous chapter (pl. 33). *The Three Brides,* a painting done two years later, that is in 1893 (pl. 38), shows perhaps even more clearly the characteristics of *Art Nouveau* in terms of a figure composition. Disregarding for the moment the mystic content of the canvas, we need only look at its long curves, the slenderness of the proportions, the flowerlike delicacy

36. Beardsley: The 'Cello Player. 1893

of bodies and limbs, the strangely slanting profiles, in order to recognize the same English sources as in Beardsley, and the same conscious effort towards a complicated, sinuous, intertwined, all-over pattern.

Again, looking back at Hodler's *The Chosen One* (pl. 34) purely from the point of view of the forms he favors, the long-drawn-out lines of the garments will be recognized as *Art Nouveau,* and the hair of the angels, the slender stem of the young tree in the middle, some of the flowers held by long delicate hands, and the tortuous movements of these hands.

Or take Munch's *The Cry* (pl. 35). The importance in it of sweeping curves as carriers of expression has already been emphasized. It is even more important in his lithograph *Madonna* (pl. 39) which was done in 1895 after a painting of 1894. The long wavy hair and the sinuous movement of the figure, the swaying lines in the background, and above all the odd frame with the embryo and the floating spermatozoa, make this work one of the most remarkable instances of *Art Nouveau* in painting, original and striking in appearance, independent of tradition, but questionable as to its wholesomeness and vital value. In Munch, a strong, sane and unsophisticated painter, this was a passing phase. He soon cast off the mannerisms of *Art Nouveau* and retained only its genuinely decorative qualities for the development of his monumental style. Incidentally, the same is true of Hodler, to whom, in a similar way, *Art Nouveau* — if we can call his style during the nineties *Art Nouveau* — was only a means of attaining the ornamental clarity of his later wall paintings and landscapes.

But *Art Nouveau* as a movement does not belong exclusively to painting, nor, indeed, is the term as a rule applied to painting at all. It means usually a short but very significant fashion in decoration, and if the works of painters and draftsmen have here been given precedence over those of architects and designers, the reason is that the new ornamental

37. Beardsley: Siegfried. 1893

fashion in the first works of its two creators appeared later than in pictures, book illustration and the like.

The two creators referred to were Louis Sullivan in Chicago and Victor Horta in Brussels.[4] Sullivan (1850–1924) was probably essentially original, Horta (1861–1947), no doubt familiar with recent English and Continental developments.[5] Sullivan's ornament remained solitary, Horta's created a craze which for a few years swept most countries on the Continent. How Sullivan came to evolve these curious tangles of tendrils, cabbagey, scalloped leaves and coral reef growths remains a mystery.[6] Can they really rest on no more promising

57

38. Toorop: The Three Brides. 1893. The Kröller-Müller Museum, Otterloo, The Netherlands

ground than Gray's *Botany*? By the time he designed the interiors of the Auditorium Building in Chicago, that is by 1888, his ornamental style was complete (pl. 40). It appears again in the Anshe Ma'ariv Synagogue of 1890–91 and at its wildest in the Carson Pirie Scott Store of 1903–04, of which, for very different reasons, more will be said later. Sullivan's ornamental ideal was an "organic decoration befitting a structure composed on broad and massive lines,"[7] and so his theory of severe functionalism discussed in a foregoing chapter cannot be understood without a careful look at his flowing ornament, nor his ornament without a vivid memory of the austerity of the main lines and blocks of his buildings.

This is what distinguishes him from Horta who remains, if not wholly, at least primarily, a decorator. Horta's *magnum opus* is his first building, the house No. 12 rue de Turin, Brussels (pl. 41). Its date is 1893, and the decoration of its interior, especially the memorable staircase, is wholly dependent on that *leitmotif* of *Art Nouveau* which has been analyzed apropos Mackmurdo's and Beardsley's and Toorop's designs. How far Horta was acquainted with these is not known, but Henry van de Velde, his most important fellow-fighter for the new ornamental style, had seen Toorop's first mature works with the keenest delight — so he told the author.

As for the relations of the young Belgians with England, van de Velde has described them thus:[8] The discovery of the English revival of craft was made by A. W. Finch (born in 1854), a painter of half-English descent who later became a potter. He bought a few things which strongly impressed his friends. That was about 1891. Shortly after, Serrurier-

39. Munch: Madonna. 1895

Bovy in Liège made the first pieces of furniture under English influence. Very soon then, so van de Velde writes, the foreign style was translated into something Belgian. In saying that, he evidently is alluding to himself. For he is completely silent about the part played by Horta and also Paul Hankar (1861—1901), the first to pick up the style of the rue de Turin.[9] While this omission no doubt detracts from the historical value of van de Velde's account, the fact remains true that his was the most comprehensive and philosophical mind amongst the young architects and designers of Belgium.

We have already met him as a theorist. As an artist he began by painting in the style of Barbizon and then of the Neo-Impressionists. It was probably when he was thirty, in 1893, that his attention was drawn to William Morris and his teachings. They made him give up painting and devote himself to applied art. He designed wall papers, brocades, decorations for books, furniture. The chairs shown in plates 42 and 43 were made for his own house at Uccle near Brussels in 1894 or 1895. They are *Art Nouveau* in the swing of their curves, but at the same time these curves are filled with a tense energy that is quite unlike the luxurious grace of Horta's lines. The ornament of genuine *Art Nouveau* is an aim in itself, that of van de Velde is meant to illustrate the function of the object or part of the object to which it is attached. Van de Velde postulates an ornamental art based on almost scientific laws of attraction and repulsion, and hence as far from arbitrariness as the creation of the engineer. Here the connection between his admiration for the machine and his own artistic style becomes visible,[10] a connection which most of his overdecorated works of about 1900 would hardly have led one to expect. And yet, at the time when his fantastic interior of Haby's barber shop in Berlin was new (1901), the public was greatly scandalized by the frank exposure of water pipes, gas pipes, and pipes for electric wiring. "You don't wear your guts like a

40. Sullivan: Auditorium Building, Chicago. 1888. Bar

watch-chain across your waistcoat either," was the comment of Berliners upon this odd mixture of functionalism and *Art Nouveau*.

In the chairs for Uccle, the functional side of van de Velde's activities is predominant. The unity of grace and energy in such objects inspired E. de Goncourt to his excellent and prophetic term "Yachting Style," which he coined when van de Velde's works were first made known to the Paris public. Van de Velde's recognition was due to S. Bing, an art dealer from Hamburg who opened a shop for modern art in the rue de Provence in 1896. Bing,

41. Horta: No. 12 rue de Turin, Brussels. 1893. Staircase

together with the German art critic Meier-Graefe, had discovered van de Velde's house at Uccle, and he invited the artist to design four rooms for his shop. The effect of this on France was immediate: furious criticism on one side, led by Octave Mirbeau in *Figaro,* and enthusiastic imitation on the other. Adversaries warned all designers against succumbing to the spell, and pointed to the excellent commercial position which French industrial art had attained by remaining faithful to eighteenth-century traditions. Convinced friends of the new style emphasized the fact that several French artists had already for some time worked

61

42 and 43. Van de Velde: Chairs for his own house in Uccle, near Brussels. 1894–95

independently on similar lines. Emile Gallé (1846–1904) in the art of glassmaking, and Auguste Delaherche (born in 1857) in the art of pottery, are the most noteworthy names. Gallé had in fact begun to exhibit glass of an utterly un-Victorian delicacy and fantastic colors as early as 1884.[11] Its shapes (pl. 44) were based on Gallé's deep belief in nature as the sole legitimate source of inspiration for the craftsman — something of the faith in the organic which we have met with in Sullivan and van de Velde.

The influence of Gallé's glass was certainly wide even before Bing opened his shop in 1896 and exhibited it consistently. For Louis Comfort Tiffany (1848–1933) had started to produce his Favrile Glass as early as 1893 (pl. 45).[12] One of Tiffany's designers, so Professor Hitchcock told the author, worked later for Bing.

Between 1895 and the early years of the twentieth century, *Art Nouveau* had as great a vogue in France as in Belgium.[13] The 1900 Exhibition in Paris was full of it. The *Métro* built its new station entrances frankly *Art Nouveau*. They were designed by Hector Guimard (1867–1942), one of the most interesting architects in the movement. He was also responsible for the Castel Béranger, a group of apartment houses at No. 16 rue La Fontaine in Passy, Paris (pl. 46). These blocks, built in 1894–98, are architecturally less rewarding than Horta's house in the rue de Turin, but equally uninhibited in their ornamental outpourings. And in furniture the fashion was as welcome to craftsmen such as Louis Majorelle (1859–1926) and Augustin Daum (1854–1909) of Nancy, and to designers such as Charles Plumet (1861–1928) (pl. 47) and Tony Selmersheim (1840–1916), as to unscrupulous manufacturers.

In exterior architecture the most remarkable contribution of *Art Nouveau* is connected with its appreciation of iron. The use of iron in façades was nothing new. (Its functional aspects will be discussed in the next chapter.) Nor were the ornamental advantages of iron

44. Gallé: Glass vase. The Museum of Modern Art, New York
45. Tiffany: Glass vases. The Museum of Modern Art, New York

for façades a discovery of the late nineteenth century. A line can indeed be drawn from the cast-iron tracery made by the Coalbrookdale Iron Company and used for instance by Porden at Eaton Hall (1803) and Eccleston Church (1809)[14] to the beginnings of ornamental cast-iron founding by the Prussian State Manufactory in 1804 which culminated in Schinkel's monument to the Berlin victims of the Napoleonic War (1821), on to the rich iron ornamentation of say the Coal Exchange by Bunning in London (1847–49)[15] and the Oxford Museum (1857–60), and so to Horta's *Maison du Peuple* in Brussels of 1896–99, Paul Saintenoy's Old England store of 1899 also in Brussels and Frantz Jourdain's *Samaritaine* store in Paris of 1905. In all these cases it was the ductile nature of the metal which fascinated designers. Horta could not have achieved the free contortions in three dimensions at the head of the staircase in No. 12 rue de Turin, if he had not used iron.

Whereas the dependence of France on Belgium in this respect as well as in all others regarding *Art Nouveau* seems now on the whole established,[16] the interesting fact about Germany is that while she also joined the movement later than Belgium, she kept surprisingly intransigent in the works of her best artists. In 1895, that is two years before an exhibition, held at Dresden in 1897, made van de Velde known in Germany, a group of young German artists had started with aims similar to his.[17] Only a few names can be given here.[18] Otto Eckmann and Hermann Obrist are the two most interesting personalities during the years 1895 to 1898. After this date, the Viennese *Sezession* took the lead. Eckmann[19] (1865–1902) had been a painter until 1894. Now he became converted, just like Morris and van de Velde. He burnt all his pictures and started as a designer. When, in 1895, Meier-Graefe succeeded in starting *Pan,* a magazine of modern art and literature in Germany, Eckmann designed the decoration of several pages (pl. 48). His ornament is completely different from Horta's and van de Velde's, and yet equally original, impressive, and repre-

63

46. Guimard: Castel Béranger,
No. 16 rue La Fontaine, Passy,
Paris. 1894–98

sentative of *Art Nouveau*: a flat pattern again, with long curves gracefully entwined, and again full of the joy of tracing many consonant lines.

But Eckmann stood on the side of Gallé and against van de Velde in his faith in nature. He does with leaves and stalks what van de Velde did by means of abstract art. This contrast between van de Velde and Eckmann and between Veldians and Eckmannites was already noticed in 1903.[20] It is not quite clear where Eckmann got his initial ideas. He did not know van de Velde when he began and probably Morris as well was unknown to him. Of connections with Gallé we have no information either. But it may be worth recording that Toorop exhibited in Munich in 1893, and that the famous Munch Exhibition in Berlin, which caused so much controversy, took place in 1892.

In 1892 Obrist (1863–1927), whose later enthusiasm for machine art has already been mentioned, was in Florence starting an embroidery workshop, which was transferred to Munich in 1894. The ornament on his cushions and hangings (pl. 49) is again less abstract than that of the Belgians and the French. But his favorite forms are only vaguely reminiscent of particular forms in nature. They recall stalks as well as shells, the indented carapaces of reptiles as well as froth and foam.[21] His influence on Endell is evident and of historic importance. Any picture of *Art Nouveau* would certainly be incomplete without a discussion of Endell. However, his contribution to the Modern Movement proper is much more essential than to *Art Nouveau*. He — and for the same reasons two more of the most fascinating *Art Nouveau* designers, Olbrich in Vienna and Mackintosh in Britain — must be left to a later chapter.

64

47. Plumet: Interior

As far as Britain is concerned, it will have been noticed that she has not yet appeared at all in this survey of *Art Nouveau* design and decoration. The reason is that, although by some of her Arts and Crafts creations she helped to form *Art Nouveau,* she kept almost consistently away from it once it had been established. Walter Crane speaks of "that strange decorative disease known as *L'Art Nouveau.*"[22] This is indeed noteworthy (and no doubt due to reasons of national character), for the functions of the Arts and Crafts in England and of *Art Nouveau* on the Continent were to a large degree the same. They are both the "Transitional" between Historicism and the Modern Movement.[23] As the Arts and Crafts in England, so *Art Nouveau* on the Continent has the merit of having revived handicraft and applied art. Undoubtedly the Arts and Crafts, in fighting for honesty of work and simplicity of form, fought for higher moral values than *Art Nouveau*. The Arts and Crafts represent a social endeavor; *Art Nouveau* is essentially art for art's sake.[24] That is what led to its ultimate failure and made it necessary for the best artists to abandon it in order to get on in the evolution of their powers. Yet *Art Nouveau* at least in one respect went beyond the Arts and Crafts. It was emphatically against any period imitation or inspiration. The Arts and Crafts were not. England, true to her innate conservatism, tried to be modern and yet keep traditions. For this reason and no other, the Modern Movement could find its valid expression only outside England.

Yet, at the time, these differences between England and the Continent were not seen by anybody. The two movements, *Art Nouveau* and the Arts and Crafts, appeared together wherever exhibitions of decorative art were held on the Continent and magazines of decorative art started.

The very fact that so many magazines suddenly appeared and so many exhibitions suddenly took place and were well attended shows the vigor of the revival on the Continent. The first of the new magazines was of course English, *The Studio,* founded in 1893, just before England's influence on the Continent set in. Amongst the artists discussed in 1893 and

65

48. Eckmann: Decoration of two pages in the magazine *Pan*. 1895

1894, the following may be noted: Beardsley, Crane, Voysey, Toorop, Khnopff. Other articles dealt with new furniture at Liberty's, the renaissance of pottery in France, the Munich *Sezession,* the New English Art Club. The first of the Continental magazines, *Pan,* came out in Germany in 1895. *Jugend* and *Simplizissimus,* both mainly satirical papers, followed in 1896. In 1897, *Art et décoration* and *L'Art décoratif* were started in France, *Deutsche Kunst und Dekoration* and *Dekorative Kunst* in Germany. Again in 1897, the *Revue des arts décoratifs* in Paris was reformed, and in Vienna one year later *Kunst und Kunsthandwerk* and *Ver Sacrum,* the magazine of the Vienna *Sezession,* began to appear.[25] Some examples of what these periodicals discussed may help to give an impression of the manifold interests at that moment. In its first years *Pan* printed poetry by Verlaine and Mallarmé, by Dehmel, Liliencron, Schlaf, illustrations by Klinger, von Hofmann, Stuck, decoration by Eckmann, Th. Th. Heine, articles on Munthe, Obrist, Tiffany. In *Dekorative Kunst* and *Deutsche Kunst und Dekoration* we find articles on English lamps, Copenhagen porcelain, Voysey, essays by Endell and Bing, illustrations of works by van de Velde, Hankar, Lemmen, Serrurier, Plumet, by Brangwyn, Ashbee, Cobden-Sanderson, and by Melchior Lechter, the illustrator of the Stefan George group. In *Art et décoration,* Horta and van de Velde are discussed, as are *La Libre esthétique* in Brussels, the English Arts and Crafts, Lalique's early glass, and furniture by Plumet and Selmersheim. At the same time *The Studio* illustrated the work of Tiffany, Plumet, Aubert, Selmersheim, and some German representatives of *Art Nouveau.*

In the history of exhibitions, England was again first in the field. The Arts and Crafts Exhibition Society showed works of artistic handicrafts in 1888, 1889, 1890, 1893, 1896. On the Continent, the most adventurous art exhibitions of that time were brought together by the group *Les XX* in Brussels, called *La Libre esthétique* since 1894.[26] They had pictures by Khnopff, Ensor, Whistler, Liebermann as early as 1884, Raffaelli, Uhde, Manzini,

49. Obrist: Embroidery. 1893

Kröyer in 1885, Monet, Renoir, Israels, Monticelli, Redon in 1886. The concurrent appearance of men like Renoir and Whistler on the one hand, and Ensor and Redon on the other, shows how strangely intermixed Impressionism and Post-Impressionism were in their action on foreign countries. In 1887 the XX had asked Sickert and Seurat to exhibit, in 1888 Toulouse-Lautrec and Signac, in 1889 Gauguin, Steer, and Klinger, in 1890 Cézanne, van Gogh, Segantini, Sisley, and Minne, in 1891 Crane and Larsson. In 1892 — an extremely telling fact — the exhibition included for the first time some stained glass, embroidery, ceramics (Delaherche), and illustrated books (Horne, Image). After this bold beginning, the exhibition of 1894 contained, besides works of Beardsley and Toorop, wallpapers and fabrics by Morris, silver by Ashbee, books of the Kelmscott Press, posters by Lautrec, and a complete studio interior furnished by Serrurier.

Only two years after this astonishingly complete show of the new tendencies, the first exhibitions on similar lines were held in Germany and France. In Germany Munich took the lead, reserving two small rooms in the Glaspalast Exhibition of 1897 for applied art. Amongst the artists represented there were Eckmann, Endell, Obrist, Th. Fischer, Dülfer, and Riemerschmid. On a larger scale was the Dresden Exhibition, held also in 1897, to which the organizers had brought whole sections of Bing's shop. This shop, which has already been mentioned more than once, marks the beginning in Paris. The date of its opening was 1896, and its name *L'Art Nouveau* gave the whole movement its name, at least in England and France. The German term *Jugendstil* was taken from the *Jugend* which, as has been said, was started in the same year 1896; and the Italian term *Stile Liberty* comes, curiously enough, from Liberty's, the furnishers' and drapers' shop, then in the Strand in London which during the nineties went in for materials and colors suitable for *Art Nouveau* schemes. So by sheer chance liberty, youth and novelty appear together in the names given to this remarkable if brief and transitory movement.

5

Engineering and Architecture in the Nineteenth Century

The Modern Movement has not grown from one root. One of its essential sources, it has been shown, was William Morris and the Arts and Crafts; another was *Art Nouveau.* The works of the nineteenth-century engineers were the third source of our present style, a source as potent as the other two.[1]

Engineering architecture in the nineteenth century was largely based on the development of iron, first as cast iron, then as wrought iron, later as steel. Towards the end of the century reinforced concrete appeared as an alternative.

The history of iron as a material of more than auxiliary usefulness in architecture begins when the inventiveness of the industrial revolution had found out how iron could be produced industrially, that is after 1750.[2] Attempts were soon made to replace timber by iron. The Grand Salon in the Louvre in Paris received its iron roof construction in 1780, the *Théâtre Français* in 1787–90, and in 1806 Napoleon wanted his Temple to the Glory of the *Grande Armée* to banish all such ephemeral materials as wood and be constructed entirely of stone and iron. Already in 1802 Ludwig Catel in Berlin had suggested an iron roof for the projected National Theatre. In London Smirke's British Museum has in its earliest part, the King's Library, iron roof beams dated 1824. The iron beams in Wilkins' University College, London, are of 1827–28. And as for churches, an iron roof went in above the stone vaults of Southwark Cathedral, also in London, probably between 1822 and 1825, and at Chartres Cathedral in 1836–41.

In all these cases iron was chosen instead of wood for purely practical, not for esthetic reasons. The same is true of the architecturally much more important development which begins with Benyon's and Bage's flax-spinning factory at Ditherington, Shrewsbury, built in 1796 (pl. 50), mentioned by Thomas Telford, the greatest of British engineers, in 1801,[3] and happily still in existence. It is five stories high, with brick walls, and inside cast-iron supports throughout, cast-iron beams, and shallow brick vaults. Timber is thus entirely avoided — obviously a tremendous advantage in a factory. The new idea — unfortunately we don't know whose it was, though we may guess at Telford himself or at John Wilkinson or Abraham Darby, the iron-masters of nearby Coalbrookdale — caught on at once. Dr. Giedion has published the designs by Boulton and James Watt for a seven-story cotton mill at Salford near Manchester, made in 1801. The names of the clients were Philips and Lee. A factory in the Stroud Valley in Gloucestershire of 1813 has been published in *The Archi-*

50. Benyon and Bage: Flax-Spinning factory, Ditherington, Shrewsbury, England. 1796

tectural Review;[4] Mr. Hamilton has given details of one built at Leeds also for Benyon's, probably by John Favey about 1816; and von Beuth, the Prussian Minister of Commerce, who traveled in England in 1823, saw plenty of factories of eight and nine stories, with paper-thin walls, iron columns and iron beams.[5]

However, as long as these members of iron remained inside, they could make little difference to the consciousness of so façade-minded a generation of architects as that of the mid-nineteenth century. The admission of iron to the front of utilitarian buildings was due to America, according to Dr. Giedion. He rediscovered the warehouses on the river front at St. Louis and discussed and illustrated examples dating from 1850 to 1877.[6] He also drew attention to James Bogardus and his pamphlet of 1856 on *Cast Iron Buildings* in which house fronts with a cast-iron frame are advocated. However, earlier still we find commercial buildings in New York making use of the same innovation, for instance on Gold Street in 1837 (pl. 51). Bogardus' building for Harper Bros. in New York dated from 1854. Professor Hitchcock draws attention to neglected British examples of the same type, especially the Jamaica Street Warehouse at Glasgow of 1855–56 (pl. 51a), an all-cast-iron structure as bold as Bogardus' and quite probably independent of him, and the Oriel Chambers at Liverpool of 1864–65. Of London George Aitchison, an architect himself busy designing commercial buildings, could say in 1864 that "one rarely sees a large building being erected without iron columns and iron girders."[8]

However, in all these structures, except perhaps for the Oriel Chambers, there is not yet the technique now current of carrying brick or masonry walls on the members of the iron skeleton. The earliest examples of regarding outer walls only as an in-filling between the

69

51. Lorillard: Building on Gold Street, New York. 1837

visible iron stanchions and beams are a shot tower in New York built about 1860–65, and a grain elevator in Brooklyn. These were, we are told, "constructed as a cast-iron framework filled in with a light wall of brick, the iron showing on the outside."[9] In Europe the warehouses of the St. Ouen Docks in Paris by Préfontaine and Fontaine were also apparently iron frame with brick used only to fill in,[10] and so was the Chocolat Menier Factory of 1871–72 at Noisiel-sur-Marne by Saulnier.

Even regarding such buildings, however, one cannot say that metal was regarded as a visual asset. It is hard to decide when this positive attitude first appeared, that is, when designers began to like the look of iron structures. One is inclined to say in iron bridges, because to us their resilience and elegance, made possible only by the use of iron, are esthetically so irresistible. This applies, to a certain degree, even to the earliest all-iron bridge ever built, the one designed in 1775 by T. F. Pritchard and built by Abraham Darby. It can still be seen at Coalbrookdale in England (pl. 52). It applies undeniably to its bolder successor,

51a. Jamaica Street Warehouse, Glasgow. 1855–56

the Sunderland Bridge, built between 1793 and 1796, designed, it seems, by Tom Paine (who, while in America between 1774 and 1787, had planned to bridge the Schuylkill River by an iron bridge). This had a span of 206 feet as against the 100 feet of Coalbrook-dale. Five years after its completion, Thomas Telford suggested replacing London Bridge with a cast-iron structure to be thrown across the river in one sleek sweep of 600 feet (pl. 53).

Parallel with this development of the arched bridge runs that of the suspension bridge. The Chinese had known bridges suspended from iron chains, and they were illustrated in Europe as early as in Kircher's *China . . . illustrata* of 1667 and in Fischer von Erlach's *Historical Architecture* of 1725. This book was translated into English in 1730, and about ten or twelve years later a bridge which made use of this Chinese principle was built across the river Tees in North England, two miles above Middleton. It was 70 feet long, but little more than 2 feet wide and chiefly crossed by miners on their way to work. The gangway was, we are told in 1794, unpleasantly restless and "few strangers dare trust themselves" on it. After this the problem of the suspension bridge seems to have been left in abeyance for sixty years, until James Finley (died in 1828) made a fresh start in America. His bridge across Jacob's Creek between Uniontown and Greenburgh had about the same length as its English predecessor and dates from 1801. Finley took a patent for suspension bridges in the same year and built eight more between that year and 1811. The longest of them crossed the cataracts of the Schuylkill and had a span of 306 feet.[11]

71

52. Darby and Wilkinson: Coalbrookdale Bridge, England. 1775–79

When England reappeared in the story of the suspension bridge, with Telford's design of 1815 for the Menai Bridge, he no doubt knew of these American developments. The Menai Bridge has a main span of 579 feet and two side spans of 260 feet each and is admirably clear in appearance. Telford was followed by Captain Samuel Brown who had taken a patent for chain bridges as early as 1817. His Union Bridge at Berwick-on-Tweed was built in 1819–20 with a main span of 449 feet. The Brighton Chain Pier followed in 1822–23 and then many others in England and on the Continent.

The most impressive of all is probably the Clifton Suspension Bridge at Bristol (pl. 54), designed in 1829–31 by Isambard Kingdom Brunel (1806–59) and begun in 1836. It seems hardly admissible that the beauty of such a structure should be purely accidental, that is the outcome of nothing but intelligent engineering. Surely, a man like Brunel must have been susceptible to the unprecedented esthetic qualities of his design — an architecture without weight, the age-old contrast of passive resistance and active will neutralized, pure functional energy swinging out in a glorious curve to conquer the 700 feet between the two banks of the deep valley. Not one word too much is said, not one compromising form introduced. The colossal simplicity of the pylons, Greek Revival in their meaning, but strangely modern in their appearance, is a superb counterpoise to the transparency of the iron construction. Only once before had such soaring spirit ruled European architecture, at the time when Amiens, Beauvais, and Cologne were built.

Brunel may not have thought of his designs in such terms, or in terms of art at all, and at that stage that was perhaps all to the good. The iron-masters certainly had ambitions of an artistic kind, and as soon as this aiming at art became a conscious effort, the results were less

53. Telford: Design for a cast-iron bridge to replace London Bridge. 1801

54. Brunel: Clifton Suspension Bridge, Bristol. Designed 1829–31. Begun in 1836

convincing. This is true of John Wilkinson's cast-iron pulpit of about 1790 at Bradley in Staffordshire and also his own proud funeral monument at Lindale near Grange-over-Sands (1808), and of that cast-iron tracery of the late eighteenth and early nineteenth century which appears in the churches of Shropshire and the surrounding counties, not too far from the Severn Valley iron-works (pl. 54a).[12]

Where iron columns occur in churches and public buildings, on the other hand, it can as a rule be said that the material was chosen for practical and not for visual reasons. Here once more England was leading. At St. Chad's in Shrewsbury by George Steuart there are two orders of slim columns encased in timber. The church is dated 1790–92.[13] Unconcealed iron appeared on a smaller scale to support galleries of theatres as well as churches. The earliest theatre recorded is Smirke's Covent Garden Theatre in London of 1808–09. The earliest churches seem to be connected with yet another fanatical iron-master, John Cragg of Liverpool, who induced young Thomas Rickman to make extensive use of iron at Everton

54a. St. Alkmund, Shrewsbury. 1795.
Cast-iron tracery

Parish Church near Liverpool in 1813–14 and at St. Michael Toxteth in 1814.[14]

A few years later as distinguished an architect as Sir John Soane recommended it in his Memorandum to the Church Commissioners of 1818,[15] but it was to be used without disguise only for smaller churches. John Nash had it quite often, though as a rule also in such a way that the public should take it for stone. Thus the Doric columns of Carlton House Terrace (begun in 1827) facing St. James' Park in London were of cast iron, and so were those of the Regent Street Quadrant (begun in 1818).[16]

However, there is at least one case in which Nash seems to have treated iron deliberately as iron and enjoyed the elegance which it can give to a support. This was in his famous extravaganza, the Pavilion at Brighton, where the main staircase is entirely of iron, and in the kitchen thin iron shafts support the ceiling. At the top copper palm leaves sprout out of them. That was in 1815 and 1818–21, respectively, important dates, since so far as we can see, they mark the first appearance of unmasked iron in connection with royalty.[17] The bulbous dome of the Pavilion also has a framework of bent iron girders. The earliest example of metal with glass in a dome was the *Halles au Blé* in Paris designed in 1809 and built in 1811. This achieved an even daylight inside the building which could not otherwise be obtained. At the same time the designers of conservatories began to realize the advantages of glass vaults. Here glass roofs had already been made use of since the beginning of the eighteenth century. The idea of "curvilinear" roofs appears for the first time in a paper read to the Horticultural Society in London by Sir G. S. Mackenzie in 1815. It was at once taken up by the horticulturist T. A. Knight of Downton Castle in Shropshire, brother of the more famous Richard Payne Knight, and by the gardener and journalist Loudon. It was

74

55. Loudon: Designs for
conservatories. 1817

Loudon who in 1817 and 1818 suggested the shapes which then became usual (above).
By 1830 there existed in England quite a number of large hothouses with curved roofs or
domes, such as the circular conservatory at Breton Hall in Yorkshire, which was 100 feet
in diameter and 60 feet high.[18] So the importance of the Paris *Jardin des Plantes* has been
rather overestimated. This was followed by the Chatsworth Conservatory which Joseph
Paxton (1801–65) built for the Duke of Devonshire in 1837–40 and which was 277 feet
long, 132 feet wide and 67 feet high.

With it the stage was set for the Crystal Palace of 1851, home of the first international
exhibition ever held, and as assertive a profession of faith in iron as the largest of the suspension bridges. But before it is reached, a few other developments must for a moment be taken
into consideration. Iron and glass have obvious advantages also for market halls and railway stations, two types of building which the fabulous growth of populations in the cities
of the early nineteenth century and the fast-growing interchange of materials and products
between factories and cities brought to the fore. The Market Hall by the Madeleine in Paris
was of an elementary iron and glass construction as early as 1824. It was not vaulted, but in
1845 Hector Horeau suggested, for the rebuilding of the Central Market Hall in Paris, a
glass vault of 300 foot span. That would have surpassed considerably the boldest of the
early English railway station vaults: those of New Street, Birmingham of 1854 by Cowper
which spanned 212 feet by means of sickle girders and then those of St. Pancras, London,
by W. H. Barlow, of 1865, with a 243 foot span.[19] The Market Hall in Paris as carried out
by Baltard & Callet in 1852–59 is also of glass and iron but not vaulted and of no special
merit.

75

In the Crystal Palace the vaults are not the determining factor either. What makes Paxton's building the outstanding example of mid-nineteenth century iron and glass architecture was rather its enormous size — 1851 feet long, that is, much longer than the palace of Versailles — and the absence of any other materials. This, even Paxton, the outsider, would probably not have ventured, if he had not worked for a temporary building. However, the fact that the Crystal Palace was re-erected in 1854 at Sydenham near London for a more permanent purpose proves that the new beauty of metal and glass had caught the fancies of progressive Victorians and of the public at large. In architectural literature there are, however, only a few who hailed Paxton's courage enthusiastically, notably that curious character, Thomas Harris, who wrote in 1862 that in the Crystal Palace "a new style of architecture, as remarkable as any of its predecessors, may be considered to have been inaugurated." And he summed up: "We may consider that iron and glass in conjunction have succeeded in giving a distinct and marked character to the future practice of architecture."[20] Ruskin was rather more doubtful of iron. He wrote on the one hand: "The time is probably near when a new system of architectural laws will be developed, adapted entirely to metallic construction," but on the other hand, he called the Crystal Palace itself nothing but "a greenhouse larger than greenhouse was ever built before" and the final proof that higher beauty was "eternally impossible" in iron.[21] In fact, the *Seven Lamps of Architecture* begins with a definition of what "separates architecture from a wasp's nest, a rat hole, or a railway station." It is quite obvious from these and many other passages that Ruskin did not know where he stood, and where architects should stand. Sir George Gilbert Scott wrote in 1858 that "it is self-evident that this triumph of modern metallic construction opens out a perfectly new field for architectural development." However, he felt that "hitherto it has usually been treated as a mere matter of engineering, and comparatively little done to bring it within the province of art." Of the use of iron in the Crystal Palace he wrote that he viewed it "as an exceptional expedient, well suited to its own purpose." Of suspension bridges he said that it "would puzzle the most ingenious bungler to render [them] unpleasing."[22]

But in spite of such qualified or unqualified appreciation of the potentialities of metal, one must not expect to find it displayed in the major works of Scott or his equally successful colleagues. Iron beams they may occasionally use, even with some architectural judgement, as for instance in Butterfield's group of buildings by All Saints, Margaret Street, London; but more than that we find very rarely. The cast-iron columns and lavish decoration of the London Coal Exchange by Bunning, 1847–49, are the most spectacular exception. Burges, fond of eccentricity, has long Early English iron piers in the Dover Town Hall, and the Oxford Museum by Deane and Woodward, 1857–60, has besides its capitals, carved by men chosen for medieval skill and conscientiousness, tall iron shafts and much iron decoration in Gothic and naturalistic forms.

But no leading architect in England was as convinced of the mission of iron as was Labrouste in France, who designed the Bibliothèque St. Geneviève in 1843 with iron shafts and iron arches inside, exposed as frankly as if he were concerned with a factory or a railway station. This progressive attitude was hailed by some and attacked by many more.

56. Boileau: St. Eugène, Paris. 1854-55

Théophile Gautier's praise of iron in 1850 — before the Crystal Palace — is more enthusiastic than anybody else's at that time. He wrote: "Mankind will produce a completely new kind of architecture . . . at the moment when the new methods created by . . . industry are made use of. The application of iron allows and enforces the use of many new forms, as can be seen in railway stations, suspension bridges and the arches of conservatories." A strange remark to come from the poet of *l'art pour l'art*. It shows the remarkable confusion between social and esthetic considerations which characterizes art criticism about the middle of the nineteenth century. Was Gautier perhaps less moved by faith in the industrial age than by delight in the forms of engineering structures and machinery, a delight such as is found also in Turner's *Rain, Steam and Speed* or Menzel's *Rolling Mill*?

Stranger still, however, is the championing of iron as a building material by Viollet-le-Duc, the restorer of so many French medieval churches and the architect of the sham medieval castle of Pierrefonds. Yet he recommended in the first volume of his *Entretiens*, written in 1859–60, that iron should be used for spanning rooms for large assemblies of people, and ten years later, in the second volume, he added a great deal more on iron. By then he pleaded thus: "Previous ages have had their several systems of construction; our age alone possesses railways, steam engines, and appliances of superior force and strength. For

57. Dutert and Contamin: *Halle des Machines*, Paris International Exhibition.
1889

what reason then do we adhere to the method of building in vogue during the last century . . . ? Why reject methods which, developed with the help of the powerful appliances
we possess, might produce novel features." Such novel features as Viollet-le-Duc designed
himself and illustrates in the *Entretiens* are curious enough, developed out of a confusion
between his clear vision that iron would allow "feats of construction hitherto unattempted"
and his unconquerable faith in the ultimate superiority of masonry. Railway stations and
market halls he calls "after all only sheds" and never appears really in sympathy with the
work of those few architects of the fifties in France who in alliance with Labrouste welcomed
iron unqualifiedly.[23]

The names to refer to are Baltard, the architect of the Market Hall, who built the church
of St. Augustin in Paris in 1860–71 with iron piers, arches and dome, and, much more
successful, L. A. Boileau (1812–96) who wrote book after book on the advantages of iron
in building and showed at St. Eugène (1854–55) and in other churches not only iron shafts
but also iron rib vaulting (pl. 56).[24]

Before we can proceed beyond the 1850's or 1860's, we must sum up. Iron had appeared
in architecture as a welcome structural material to be used but not to be displayed — and it
was still used in that spirit for the construction say of the dome of the Washington Capitol
in 1855–65. Where it appeared in the exterior of buildings in other than ornamental con-
texts, its function was also partly utilitarian — for instance in the St. Louis river front and
the warehouses and office buildings of London, Liverpool and Glasgow. Inside buildings
again iron was not usually chosen because of a special liking for it, in spite of Nash and
later Labrouste and Boileau. An esthetically high standard was only very occasionally

58. Eiffel: Eiffel Tower, Paris. 1889

achieved by it. If we want to see iron and steel at their best, unhampered by convention and tradition, we must go to the bridges, those of the early nineteenth century, and then, on a scale ever growing, to the Brooklyn Bridge of 1870–83 with its main span of 1596 feet and the Firth of Forth Bridge of 1883–89 with its 1735 foot span, or we must go to the iron and glass vaults, to St. Pancras and after that to the miracle of nineteenth-century vaulting, the *Halle des Machines* at the Paris International Exhibition of 1889 (pl. 57). This had a height of 150 feet, a length of 1400 feet, and a span of 385 feet; it must have conveyed an un-precedented feeling of space and weightlessness. The illustration shows the fascinating

59. Sullivan: Wainwright Building, St. Louis. 1890–91

ease with which the steel arms spring from the supporting shafts. The pairs of arms are not joined together at the top of the vault; they just touch each other by means of the same narrow bolts used at the bottom of the shafts.

Dutert was the architect, and Contamin the engineer of this hall.[25] Their names are hardly known to historians of architecture. The healthy state of anonymity, a matter of course in medieval building, is preserved here, while it was lost in architecture, owing first to the Renaissance and then to the Romantic conception of the artist and his individual

60. Burnham and Root: Monadnock Block, Chicago. 1890–91

genius. Even now, Scott, Garnier, and Semper are better known than Telford and Brunel, Polenceau, Horeau, and Henri de Dion. The only engineer whose name has remained famous is Gustave Eiffel (1832–1923), and in this case it is the name of one work which has made it immortal. Eiffel erected the Eiffel Tower for the same International Exhibition of 1889 for which the *Halle des Machines* was built. He had already tried out the construction of those sickle-shaped girders that form the base of the tower, in several bridges which are among the boldest of the century, for instance the Duoro Bridge (1875) and the Garabit

Viaduct (1879). The overwhelming effect of the Eiffel Tower (pl. 58) depends on its height of 1000 feet — unsurpassed until after the First World War — and also on the elegance of its curved outline, and the powerful yet controlled energy of its *élan*.

The Eiffel Tower would not have been erected and become the idol of the Parisian and the foreign visitor, if steel by then, that is by 1890, had not been established. So from 1890 on, the most advanced architectural thought and the visual qualities of progressive buildings can no longer be fully understood without taking steel into consideration. In Europe its first effect on the esthetics of architecture has already found mention in the preceding chapter: the all-glass façades of Horta's *Maison du Peuple* of 1896–99 and the buildings following its example. In America the effect was even more fundamental and influential. It is connected with the coming of the skyscraper.

Nowadays, we no longer call every tall building a skyscraper. The definition which has become accepted makes the essential quality of the skyscraper a steel skeleton with outer and inner walls functioning only as screens. Recent research has established with great precision the various stages which converted the tall office building with weight-bearing walls into the skyscraper.[26] They do not concern us here in detail.

All that need be said of the prehistory of the skyscraper is that tall office buildings were not possible before the advent of the elevator (1852) and more particularly the electric elevator (invented by W. von Siemens in 1880). A height of 349 feet was reached, in spite of solid masonry walls, by the Pulitzer Building in New York in 1888–89. Meanwhile, however, the Home Insurance Building in Chicago by William Le Baron Jenney (1832–1907) had been erected in 1884–85 with a genuine skeleton construction, and other Chicago office blocks such as the Tacoma Building of 1887–88 by Holabird and Roche improved Jenney's innovation at once.[27] But in their appearance neither the Home Insurance nor the Tacoma Building nor the other earliest Chicago skyscrapers show features in advance of the customary masonry towers put up before. It was left to Sullivan to pay attention to the voice of steel. The result is the Wainwright Building in St. Louis (pl. 59), a milestone in the evolution of the Modern Movement. It was designed in 1890. Mr. Morrison has pointed out rightly that its façades do not by any means show its construction in its entirety. The masonry strips at the corners are still wider than the other uprights and all uprights are of the same width, although only every second of them corresponds to a steel stanchion. The top story with its bull's-eyes and the far projecting top cornice with its lush Sullivanian *Art Nouveau* decoration also are reminiscent of stone traditions. Yet Sullivan had understood that the grid of steel calls for an exterior essentially based on one and the same unit, or, as he put it, that we must "take our cue from the individual cell, which requires a window with its separating pier, its sill and lintel, and without more ado, make them all look alike, because they all are alike."[28] Hence the splendid simplicity of rhythm and the unfaltering directness of effect. In contrast to van de Velde, Sullivan thus translated into the reality of big buildings those revolutionary theories of his which we have discussed at the beginning of this book.

Nor was he the only architect in Chicago to have such a strong feeling for the character of the coming century. It appeared in Richardson when he was faced with the job of design-

61. De Baudot: St. Jean de Montmartre, Paris. Begun in 1894

ing the Marshall Field Wholesale Building in 1885, a massive block, not a skyscraper at all, but a monument to commerce and industry erected regardless of all the paraphernalia traditionally connected with monumentality. Its round arches are the only allusion to the architect's Neo-Romanesque past. The spirit is wholly original, and must have impressed enormously not only Sullivan but also Burnham and Root, when they built the Monadnock Block in 1890–91 (pl. 60). This building has neither any Richardsonian forms nor does it make use of a steel skeleton. It is the last of the big masonry towers, yet in its uncompromising refusal to mitigate its sheer lines by any moldings and any ornament, it is entirely of the new age. To that extent can technique and esthetics be at variance at any one moment even in so consistent a development as that of the Chicago School.

In the cellars of the Monadnock Block and other American office buildings concrete was used, though not as a feature of architectural design. Actually, the strengthening of building foundations was one of the first tasks to be entrusted to this new material, which was to become so significant for the twentieth century. To complete this chapter on the achievements of the engineer before 1900, a few facts about the invention and early application of ferro-concrete must be given.[29] The first patent was taken out by Monier in 1867. It concerned the use of a kind of ferro-concrete for plant-pots. In the same year Coignet adopted the new composition for the cellars of the Paris Exhibition buildings. The next step was the introduction of concrete into building proper. The scientific experiments and calculations leading to the use of concrete for girders are mainly due to two German engineers, Wayss (1884) and Koenen (1886). They endeavored to find the disposition of iron and artificial stone which would make the best use of the distinctive qualities of both. Proceeding consistently from this research, Hennebique arrived in 1892 at his patent for compound beams — a system of molding in one piece the supporting girders and the beams across the ceiling. Further patents followed until, from 1900 on, concrete became a serious competitor to steel. The first building of which the effect is based entirely on concrete is Anatole de Baudot's church of St. Jean de Montmartre, begun in 1894 (pl. 61). As it stands today, it is proof not only of its designer's audacity — for in church architecture there is always a special resistance to innovations — but also of his outstanding sense of spatial possibilities. The treatment of piers, arches and ribs may have its source in the use made of iron by Boileau, yet the bareness and sheerness of the supports, the unmitigated scaffolding effect of the concrete beams passing forward and backward and across, and the glazing of pendentives and lantern achieve an austere directness which may well be called Gothic, while at the same time heralding the spatial intricacies of Mackintosh and Le Corbusier. Between the completion of this building and the present day, France has remained the leader in the development of concrete architecture.

One more remark is necessary before this account of engineering architecture can be closed. Ruskin, Morris, and their followers hated the machine and consequently the new steel and glass architecture, which, according to Ruskin, is "eternally separated from all good and great things by a gulf which not all the tubular bridges nor engineering of ten thousand nineteenth centuries cast into one great bronze-foreheaded century, will ever overpass one inch of."[30]

Ruskin's reasons for this frantic scorn were of a primarily esthetic nature, those of Morris were entirely social. Morris was unable to appreciate the positive possibilities of the new materials, because he was too intensely concerned with the negative consequences of the industrial revolution. He saw only what had been destroyed: craftsmanship and pleasurable work. But no new period in human civilization has ever arisen without an initial phase in which a complete upheaval of values took place; and such phases are not especially pleasant for contemporaries.

The engineers, on the other hand, were too absorbed in their thrilling discoveries to notice the social discontent accumulating around them, and to listen to Morris' warning voice. Owing to this antagonism, the two most important tendencies in nineteenth-century art and architecture could not join forces. The Arts and Crafts kept their retrospective attitude, the engineers their indifference to art as such.

The leaders of *Art Nouveau* were the first to understand both sides. They accepted the new gospel of artistic service preached by Morris, but they also accepted our new age as the machine age. This is one of their lasting titles to fame.

It is essential to understand the Modern Movement as a synthesis of the Morris Movement, the development of steel building, and *Art Nouveau*. The account of these three principal lines of progress, which has been given in this and the preceding chapters, will now enable us to devote the remaining pages of this book to the Modern Movement itself, as it grew in England, the United States, and on the Continent.

6

England, Eighteen-ninety to Nineteen-fourteen

We must now return to English architecture and design. At the end of the eighties, as was shown, Morris was the leader in design, Norman Shaw in architecture. The deliberate break with tradition, which characterized the style of Europe's greatest painters about 1890 and the style of the initiators of *Art Nouveau,* was not made and not desired in England. So it seemed appropriate to leave until now the discussion of the English development from 1890 onwards, though at least one English architect had ventured on a new style of an original and highly stimulating nature, before *Art Nouveau* had begun. This was C. F. Annesley Voysey (1857–1941).[1] It has already been said that his designs were a source of inspiration to *Art Nouveau.* Van de Velde told the author of the revolutionizing effect of Voysey's wallpapers on him and his friends.[2] His words were: "It was as if Spring had come all of a sudden." And indeed we have only to look at one of Voysey's wallpapers printed in the nineties (pl. 62) and one of his somewhat later printed linens (pl. 63), to see the great difference between him and Morris. Not that he aimed at novelty; his modifications and progressiveness, it would seem, were almost unconscious. Doctrines and hard-and-fast rules were not his way. In the controversy between supporters of stylized and of naturalistic orna- ment, he did not take sides. For although, in an interview in 1893, he declared realism to be unsuitable for decoration, he was inclined to admit plants and beasts in patterns on condition that they be "reduced to mere symbols." This may seem in accord with Morris, but there is a distinctly new note in Voysey's urgent desire to "live and work in the present."[3]

So he arrives at patterns which are happily near to nature, and at the same time full of decorative charm. The graceful shapes of birds flying, drifting, or resting, and of tree-tops, with or without leaves, are favorite motifs of Voysey's, and there is an unmistakable kind- liness in his childlike stylized trees and affectionately portrayed birds and beasts. A com- parison between these wallpapers or linens and Morris' *Honeysuckle* (pl. 6) shows what a decisive step has been taken away from nineteenth-century "historicism" into a new world of light and youth.

It is known that everywhere in English cultural life a longing for fresh air and gaiety expressed itself at the end of Queen Victoria's reign. The success of Liberty's about 1890 depended largely on their Eastern silks in delicate shades and their other Chinese imports. The history of the part played by China and Japan in European art since 1860 has not yet been written. It would be very interesting to show the influence of the East appearing here in a loose technique of painting, there in the greatest finesse of line and contours, there again in clear, soft and pure color, and in yet other works in flat pattern effects. Owing to the unique synthesis of ornamental and "Impressionist" qualities in Eastern art, both the Impressionists and, at the opposite pole, the originators of *Art Nouveau,* could use what Japanese woodcuts and Chinese pottery had to teach them. The Impressionist went to Japan for a lightness that he took for *plein air,* for a sketchy handling of the brush, and a flatness of surfaces, which he wrongly interpreted as meaning the shadelessness of strong sunlight. His adversary, more justly, stressed the high degree of stylization in every line drawn and every surface decorated by an Eastern artist. That is why Japanese woodcuts can appear in the backgrounds of Manet's *Zola* and Degas' *Tissot* as well as van Gogh's *Père Tanguy* and Ensor's *Skeleton Studying Eastern Paintings.* The case of Whistler is especially instructive; for it proves that in the same painter at the same time both aspects of the Eastern style might be reflected. The influence of Eastern color, Eastern delicacy, and Eastern composition on his yet so clearly Impressionist portraits is evident and has no need of the Chinese costume in the *Princesse du Pays de la Porcelaine* to stress it.[4] At the same time however, Whistler could make this same picture the chief accent of a room decorated in a style which, although not free from traces of "historicism," obviously pointed forward to *Art Nouveau.*[5] Moreover Whistler was the first artist to plead for rooms with completely plain walls in light colors. In 1878, he decorated his own house in Tite Street, Chelsea, in a scheme the principal effects of which were white and rich yellow walls, some pieces of Chinese porcelain, and a few simply framed pictures and etchings.[6] In trying to imagine such rooms, we feel ourselves at once in the early years of the twentieth century, no longer in the days of Morris and Ruskin. And yet, in theory (if that is not too heavy an expression for his casual *aperçus*) and in technique, Whistler was as complete an Impressionist as anybody, and therefore an object of passionate hatred to those who worked for a new outlook on life and art.[7] There is no need to go again into that unpleasant case, Whistler versus Ruskin. Morris was bound to follow Ruskin. This was a matter of principle primarily, but also a matter of taste. The man who regarded Burne-Jones as the great living painter of the late Victorian era could certainly not appreciate Whistler's superficial (truly superficial) pictorial impressions.[8]

One would expect to find the same contrast between the disciples of the Arts and Crafts and the Impressionists as between Morris and Whistler. However, it is a fact which has already been mentioned in connection with the exhibitions of *Les XX,* that on the Continent the introduction of Impressionism, and of the new decorative style in both its forms, as Arts and Crafts and as *Art Nouveau,* took place concurrently and were both due to the same persons. Meier-Graefe, who was one of the first to discover van de Velde, wrote books on Renoir and Degas, and also on van Gogh and Gauguin. And even today most people interested in art are unaware of the irreconcilable difference between Impressionism as a doctrine and the doctrine of Morris and all his followers. Yet, it is so obvious that the antithesis, Impressionism versus Arts and Crafts, is but the artistic expression of a far more comprehensive cultural antithesis between two generations. On the one side there is a conception of art as a rapid rendering of momentary surface effects, on the other as an expression of what is final and essential; on the one side there is the philosophy of Art for Art's sake, on the other a renewed faith in a social message of art. The Impressionists stand for the

62. Voysey: Design for a wallpaper. c.1895

63. Voysey: *Stags and Trees*, printed linen. 1908

exquisite luxuries of late nineteenth-century Paris, the Arts and Crafts for "roughing it" in the spirit of that Youth Movement which is so significant for the years around 1900 and after, and can be traced in Bergson as much as in the foundation of the first reformed public schools in England: Abbotsholme (1889) and Bedales (1892).

In design, Voysey is the outstanding but by no means the only representative of this new *joie de vivre*. Some of Crane's late wallpapers also depart from Morris' heaviness. Brangwyn's (born in 1867) designs for textiles are another example. In comparing one of his rugs (pl. 65) with those by Morris, one recognizes the tendency towards large, unbroken surfaces,

64. Voysey: Cruet set and toast rack

65. Brangwyn: Rug

66. Voysey: The Orchard, Chorley Wood, Buckinghamshire, England. 1900

strong colors, bold patterns — a parallel to Cézanne or Gauguin in painting. As long as Continental architects believed in *Art Nouveau,* it was chiefly English designs for wallpapers, printed linens, chintzes and so on which appealed to them. As soon as the new desire for *Sachlichkeit* spread, all the pioneer work done by the English architects and artists in the shaping (not the decoration) of objects became topical. It must have been a delightful surprise to those who — like Muthesius — came to England, weary of the license of *Art Nouveau,* to see a toast-rack or a cruet set designed by Voysey (pl. 64). The refreshing simplicity of his wallpapers is also the keynote of these small things of everyday use. Their charm lies solely in the cleanness and gracefulness of their shapes.

Of particular importance for the coming Modern Movement was the expression of this new spirit in furnishing. The entrance hall of Voysey's own home, The Orchard, Chorley Wood, Buckinghamshire, of 1900 can serve as an example (above), with its lightness: the woodwork painted white, a pure intense blue for the tiles, unmitigated contrasts of uprights and horizontals, especially in the screen to the staircase (a motif which was for a time to become eminently popular), and furniture of bold, direct if a little *outrés* forms. Somewhat later, in a bench made for Garden Corner, Chelsea, London in 1906 (pl. 68) even these reminiscences of *Art Nouveau* have gone, and the whole design, with the exception of the brackets to the small side flaps, consists entirely of vertical and horizontal members. And as for the brackets, they have the elementary geometric shape of exact quarter circles. The material is unpolished and unstained oak, another instance of the "back to fundamentals" and "back to nature" tendencies which stand at the beginning of our century.

There is one more thing which must be said about Voysey and which places him further from Morris and close to us. He was a designer, not a craftsman. He could not in fact, so he told the author, work in any craft. Ernest Gimson (1864–1920),[9] the greatest of the English artist-craftsmen, was, as a matter of fact, in not too different a position, although

89

not many people realize it. He had been trained, it is true, in craftsmanship, but his famous works of cabinetmaking, metal-work and so on are only designed and not made by him. The chairs shown here (pl. 67) give an impression of his honesty, his feeling for the nature of wood, and his unrevolutionary spirit. Few of his works have this superb simplicity. As a rule, Gimson was more responsive to English tradition and did not despise the use of forms invented in the past.

On a really commercial basis good progressive furniture was at the same time made by Sir Ambrose Heal (born in 1872). The firm of Heal & Son had been producing Victorian furniture, until Ambrose Heal changed its course. A wardrobe which Heal's showed at the Paris Exhibition of 1900 (pl. 69) has the same brightness which we found in Voysey's wallpapers. Plain surfaces of slightly fumed and waxed oak contrast with small panels decorated in pewter and ebony. There are no long curves; the patterns are composed of

67. Gimson: Chairs. 1901

68. Voysey: Bench. 1906

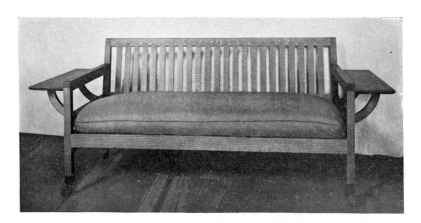

69. Heal: Wardrobe. 1900

rectangles and gracefully drawn little flowers. The close atmosphere of medievalism has vanished. Living amongst such objects, we breathe a fresher air.

Even more important historically than such exhibition pieces of Heal's was their production for the ordinary market. In 1898, the first catalog of Heal's Plain Oak Furniture came out and started the revival of the simple wooden bedstead in England.[10] For more than twenty years these pleasant bedsteads were popular in the English furniture trade, until they were swept away by misguided supporters of modernistic forms.

Exactly the same contrast between 1890 and 1900 as in cabinetmaking is to be found in English printing. Morris' Kelmscott Press — founded in 1890 — produced pages the effect of which depends largely on their exquisite, medievalist decoration. Cobden-Sanderson's and Emery Walker's Doves Press — founded in 1900 and mentioned in this book on page 17 — secured for the plain unadorned type face its place in modern book production.

As far as English architecture is concerned, the historical position is not quite so simple as in applied art. It has been pointed out that, by 1890, Norman Shaw had attained a style which, based on Queen Anne, was so "modern" in character and so perfectly suited to English needs and taste that it could hardly be improved on, as long as no open break with tradition was attempted. The earliest and most remarkable cases of independence — earlier

70. Mackmurdo: The architect's house, Enfield, Middlesex, England. Before 1880

in fact than that of Horta — are afforded by some of the early architectural works of Mack-murdo and Voysey. Mackmurdo's house at Enfield (above) built before 1880 is of a surprisingly free carriage. The flat roof and the few horizontal windows of the second floor are particularly noteworthy. In 1886 he put up a stand for the products of his own guild at an exhibition at Liverpool (below). The attenuated shafts with their excessive top cornices instead of capitals and the repetition of these odd forms on top of the fascia board are even more original and started a fashion when Voysey and then several others took them up. Of Mackmurdo's strong influence on Voysey there can be no doubt. He himself said to the au-

71. Mackmurdo: Exhibition stand, Liverpool. 1886

72. Voysey: Nos. 14 and 16, Hans Road, Kensington, London. 1891
73. Voysey: House in Bedford Park, near London. 1888

thor that when he was very young Mackmurdo had impressed him even more than Morris. Yet the first house which Voysey designed, the one in The Parade at Norman Shaw's garden suburb Bedford Park near London (pl. 73), is amazingly independent, considering the date, 1888. The arrangement of the windows is particularly striking. But whereas this kind of free grouping also prevails in the works of Norman Shaw and his school, the whiteness of the walls was an open protest against the surrounding red brick of Shaw's garden suburb. The tower-like tallness of the house also and the skipping rhythm of bare walls and horizontal window openings were innovations introduced deliberately and not without a youthful sense of mischief.

However, Voysey did not go on in that direction, or else he would have developed into an architect of *Art Nouveau*. Already in the tiny studio built in St. Dunstan's Road, West Kensington, London, in 1891 (pl. 74), the general proportions are closer to English traditions, cottage traditions, than anything in the house in Bedford Park, although the detail is again remarkably novel, above all the massive chimney, the batter of the buttresses on the right and also the ironwork in front (obviously inspired by Mackmurdo's woodwork in 1886). In the same year Voysey designed two houses in Hans Road, Kensington, London (pl. 72). Here the style of Bedford Park still lingers in the porch and the scrolled-up parapet. But the two little oriel windows are borrowed from Norman Shaw, and altogether the houses, looked at today, do not impose their individuality against the Norman Shaw style as consistently as did the Bedford Park house.

When Voysey began to get commissions for houses in the country, his appreciation of English traditions was decisively strengthened. A man of intense feeling for nature, as his

74. Voysey: Studio, St. Dunstan's Road, West Kensington, London. 1891

designs prove him to have been, he could not but think of his houses in conjunction with the surrounding countryside, and so shapes offered themselves which were more akin to the English manor house and cottage of the past than to those he had evolved in London. His country-house practice began in the early nineties and by 1900 had assumed very large dimensions. He never built a church, never a public building and only once a small warehouse.

Perrycroft, Colwall, Malvern Hills, dates from 1893 (pl. 75). It is typical of Voysey's ideas of what a country house should be like. In spite of such strikingly modern features as the consistently horizontal fenestration and the massive block shapes of the chimney stacks, it is nowhere demonstratively anti-traditional, and it fits perfectly with its natural surroundings (a garden was planned and planted together with the house) and the architectural character of the country.

This is even more evident in another building, the house erected for Canon L. Grane at Shackleford in Surrey, in 1897 (pl. 76). Today it is not easy to appreciate the candor and simplicity of its façade. For, in Britain at least, it has become too much of a standard example ineptly imitated by hundreds of speculative builders all along the arterial roads and all over the suburbs. However, from the historian's point of view, it remains no small feat to have created the pattern for the vast majority of buildings carried out over a period of thirty years and more. What was not copied from Voysey, needless to say, was what impresses us today as his most progressive motifs — the long, drawn-out window strips and the completely bare triangles of the gables, broken only in one place by a charmingly tiny and just a trifle precious window.

This introduction of an occasional effect of *Art Nouveau* piquancy helps a great deal to lighten the otherwise puritan honesty of many of Voysey's houses. Thus for instance in the

94

75. Voysey: Perrycroft, Colwall, Malvern Hills, England. 1893

76. Voysey: House for Canon L. Grane, Shackleford, Surrey, England. 1897

77. Voysey: Lodge and stables, Merlshanger, near Guildford, Surrey, England. 1895

78. Smith and Brewer: Mary Ward Settlement, Tavistock Place, London. 1895

lodge to Merlshanger on the Hogsback near Guildford, Surrey, designed in 1896 (pl. 77) the typical Voysey buttresses and far projecting eaves carry a very flat curved cupola with a spirelet, needle-thin and ending in a weather vane. In the same way in one of his most successful country houses, Broadleys on Lake Windermere (pls. 79 and 80) of 1898 the eaves cornice is supported once again by thin iron brackets and their delicacy adds a touch of lightness to the whole front.

But such effects are only a little light relief in what is otherwise sound, balanced, vigorous design without any tendency to demonstrative novelty. That is what makes the water front of Broadleys so impressive. Here, one sees clearly, was a mind equally averse to the picturesque tricks of the Shaw school and the preciousness of *Art Nouveau*. From this center bay with its completely unmolded mullions and transoms, from these windows cut clean and sheer into the wall, access to the architectural style of today could have been direct, more direct probably than from the designs of those few in England who in the late nineties appeared more revolutionary than Voysey. Whom should one count amongst them? Maybe Baillie Scott (1865–1945) who started a little later than Voysey and very much under his influence,[11] and C. R. Ashbee, whose writings and social activities have been mentioned before and whose most original houses, in Cheyne Walk, Chelsea, London, date from only a few years after 1900.[12] Far more remarkable historically is the Mary Ward Settlement in Tavistock Place, London (above) built in 1895 by Dunbar Smith (1866–1933) and Cecil Brewer (1871–1918). Its relation to Norman Shaw (Venetian window) as well as to Voysey (top parts of the projecting wings) is evident. The rhythm of the blocks on the other hand, the proportions of the recessed center part with its blank brick wall and the high bare cornice, the wide projection of the roofs, all point distinctly forward to the style of

79 and 80. Voysey: Broadleys on Lake Windermere, England. 1898

today, and the asymmetrically projecting porch is freer and more "organic" in treatment than Voysey ever wanted to be.[13]

This particular feature in its turn must have impressed the older C. Harrison Townsend (1850–1928) whose principal work, the Whitechapel Art Gallery, London, dates from 1897–99 (pl. 82). But Townsend's style is of more complex origins. The deliberate lack of symmetry between ground floor and upper floor, as well as the long row of surprisingly low windows and the leaf ornament of the friezes, ultimately point no doubt to Voysey, but the heavy arch above the entrance must reflect some knowledge on Townsend's part of what Richardson had done in America for twenty years and more.[14] If this assumption is cor-

81. Townsend: Horniman Museum, London. 1900–02

rect, we have here the first case of American influence on England. The two flat friezes above the row of windows also conjure up some memories of, say, Richardson's Brattle Square Church in Boston of 1870–72, and the American connection became more distinct with Townsend's next building, the Horniman Museum in South London of 1900–02 (above). The robust square tower with its rounded corners and stumpy top is utterly different from the elegant spirelets which Voysey and his imitators adored so much. Townsend's designs during these years, in spite of all that it might be possible to say about

82. Townsend: Whitechapel Art Gallery, London. 1897–99

sources in England and abroad, are without question the most remarkable example of a reckless repudiation of tradition among English architects of the time. Among English, not among British architects. For in Glasgow there worked during these very years a group of artists as original and as imaginative as any in Europe. In painting, the Glasgow Boys, Guthrie, E. A. Walton, Lavery, Henry, Hornel and so on are well enough known. Their first exhibition abroad impressed Europe considerably. But in design and decoration the first appearance of the Glasgow school at an exhibition in Vienna was a revelation.

83. Mackintosh: Art School, Glasgow. 1907–09. Interior of library

The center of the group was Charles Rennie Mackintosh (1868–1928) with his wife
Margaret Macdonald and her sister Mrs. McNair.[15] In dealing with him, we are able at last
to link up the development in England with the main tendency of Continental architecture
in the nineties, with *Art Nouveau*. Before he was twenty-eight, Mackintosh was chosen to
design the new building for the Glasgow Art School, 1898–99 (pl. 84). Not a single feature
here is derived from period styles. The façade is of a strongly personal character and, in
many ways, leads on to the twentieth century, although the entrance bay with balcony and
short turret is deliberately fantastical and not unlike Townsend's contemporary work. But
the rest of the front is extremely simple, almost austere in its bold uniform fenestration. In
the horizontal windows of the offices on the ground floor and the high studio windows on
the second floor, no curves are admitted; unbroken upright lines prevail even in the railing
in front of the building, counteracted only by a few lighter and more playful *Art Nouveau*

ornaments at the top. The same contrast exists between the rigidity of the second-floor windows and the strange metal stalks at their base, functionally justified for putting planks on to facilitate window cleaning. However, be that as it may, this row of metal lines reveals one of Mackintosh's most important qualities, his intense feeling for spatial values. Our eyes have to pass through the first layer of space, indicated by the metal brackets, before arriving at the solid stone front of the building. The same transparency of pure space will be found in all of Mackintosh's principal works.

The ground plan of the building is clear and lucid, showing in another light the architect's interest in space, an interest rare among artists of *Art Nouveau*. One more instance may be given to prove that this is really the keynote of Mackintosh's creation: the interior of the library of the Glasgow Art School, which forms the center room of the west wing, planned

84. Mackintosh: Art School, Glasgow. 1898–99

85. Mackintosh: Cranston Tearoom, Ingram Street, Glasgow. 1907–11. Interior

in 1907 (pl. 83). The simple motif of a high room with aisles and galleries around three sides is so enriched that the resulting impression is an overwhelmingly full polyphony of abstract form. The galleries do not project far enough to reach the pillars which separate "nave" from "aisles." Horizontal beams are inserted to connect the walls with the pillars and to support the galleries. Airy balustrades, *Art Nouveau* in detail, run from the parapets of the gallery to the pillars. Their sole purpose is to offer interesting perspectives. Curves, rare and all the more expressive in Mackintosh's earlier work, have now completely disappeared. Uprights and horizontals, squares and oblongs determine the effect. This and the number of fascinating vistas which the architect has achieved here and in another principal work of the same period, the Cranston Tearoom in Ingram Street, 1907–11 (above), show him as the European counterpart of Frank Lloyd Wright and one of the few true forerunners of the most ingenious juggler with space now alive: Le Corbusier. Le Corbusier once confessed that his desire in building is to create poetry. Mackintosh's attitude is very similar. Building in his hands becomes an abstract art, both musical and mathematical.

The façade of the west wing of the Art School is an instance of this. Here the abstract artist is primarily concerned with the shaping of volume and not of space, of solids not of voids (pl. 86). The esthetic value of the straight slender shafts into which the windows are inserted is entirely independent of their function. The contrasts between fretwork and solid ashlar, and between the menacing bareness on the left and the complex polyphony on the right, are also effects more comparable to abstract relief than to buildings of Voysey's kind.

A glance at the earlier and the later part of the Art School reveals the development of Mackintosh's taste between 1897 and 1907. Delicate metal ornament of linear appeal is no

86. Mackintosh: Art School, Glasgow. 1907–09. Library wing

longer used. A squareness and robustness prevail which come as a surprise. They are, it seems certain, Mackintosh's way of admitting national tradition. His links with the Scottish baronial past are perhaps more evident in his country houses than in a public building such as the Art School. If we look at the general form and outline of the Blackie house in Helensburgh of 1902, the round turret, the steep gable, the massive chimney stacks are unmistakable (pl. 88). Once that has been recognized, a building like the Scotland Street School in Glasgow of 1904 (pl. 87) will at once reveal the same sympathies. Even the library wing of the Art School will now show its baronial relations, perched as it is on the steep slope of the street leading up the front.[16] Its great fascination is in fact its synthesis of traditional elements with a remarkable fearlessness in the functional distribution of the windows and the

87. Mackintosh: Scotland Street School, Glasgow. 1904

weird harshness of its narrow angular upright forms. Dutch architects of the 1920's must have derived much benefit from this building.

However, the question of Mackintosh's connections with the Continent is a complicated one and demands a rather more detailed discussion. The obvious similarity between Mackintosh's earliest interior designs — or one should rather say the interior designs of Mackintosh and Margaret Macdonald — and the style of the Viennese *Sezession* has often been commented on. The Cranston Tearoom in Buchanan Street of 1897–98 (pl. 90) should be studied in this connection — incidentally the first monument of the British Tearoom Movement, a movement in its opposition to the snugness and stuffiness of the tavern again typical of the new desire for health, light and freshness. In the Buchanan Street tearoom the walls are decorated with the same long and graceful lines and the same excessively slim figures which we find in the works of Klimt and his followers. But the tearoom dates from 1897, and in that year, Klimt's manner was still dependent on that of the earlier draftsmen of *Art Nouveau* (pl. 89). One year later, in 1898, when the *Sezession* started their periodical *Ver Sacrum,* its pages were decorated in a style strikingly similar to Mackintosh's. As *The Studio* had published some designs for the Cranston Tearoom in 1897, one can safely conclude that the change of taste in the artists of the *Sezession* was at least partly caused by impressions received from Mackintosh's work. This hypothesis is confirmed by the fact that, in 1900, the *Sezession* in Vienna invited Mackintosh to show work at their annual exhibition in Vienna.[17] What was so thrilling to the artists of Vienna in his display when it was up and on show, has been formulated very well by Ahlers-Hestermann: "Here was indeed the oddest mixture of puritanically severe forms designed for use, with a truly lyrical evaporation of all interest in usefulness. These rooms were like dreams, narrow panels, grey silk, very very slender wooden shafts — verticals everywhere. Little cupboards of rectangular shape and with far projecting top cornices, smooth, not of visible frame-and-panel construction; straight, white and serious-looking, as if they were young girls

88. Mackintosh: Blackie house, Helensburgh, near Glasgow. 1902

ready to go to their first Holy Communion — and yet not really; for somewhere there was a piece of decoration like a gem, never interfering with the contour, lines of hesitant elegance, like a faint distant echo of van de Velde. The fascination of these proportions, the aristocratically effortless certainty with which an ornament of enamel, colored glass, semi-precious stone, beaten metal was placed, fascinated the artists of Vienna who were already a little bored with the eternal solid goodness of English interiors. Here was mysticism and asceticism, though by no means in a Christian sense, but with much of a scent of heliotrope, with well-manicured hands and a delicate sensuousness. . . . As against the former overcrowding, there was hardly anything in these rooms, except that, say, two straight chairs, with backs as tall as a man, stood on a white carpet and looked silently and spectrally at each other across a little table. . . . 'Chambres garnies pour belles âmes' is what Meier-Graefe wrote."

Ideal evidence of these intentions was the house which Mackintosh designed for a competition of the German publisher Koch in 1901 (pl. 91). Here everything can be seen that Ahlers-Hestermann is talking about and it can also be seen clearly enough that Mackintosh's sources are Voysey, Beardsley, Toorop.[18] This synthesis of their style was the legacy of Britain to the coming Modern Movement. No other British contribution to European architecture before the First World War carries enough weight to be discussed here.[19] For various reasons England forfeited her leadership in the shaping of the new style just about 1900, that is, at the very moment when the work of all the pioneers began to converge into one universal movement. One reason was given in Chapter 1:[20] the leveling tendency of the coming mass movement — and a true architectural style *is* for every man — was too much against the grain of the English character. A similar antipathy prevented the ruthless scrapping of traditions which was essential to the achievement of a style fitting our century. So, at the very moment when Continental architects discovered the elements of a genuine

89. Klimt: Tragedy. 1897

style for the future in English building and English crafts, England herself receded into an eclectic Neo-Classicism, of great dignity sometimes, but with hardly any bearing on present-day problems and needs. For country houses and town houses Neo-Georgian or Neo-Colonial became popular; in public buildings, banks and so on, solemn rows of colossal columns reappeared, not entirely free from the influence of the United States where, after the Chicago Exhibition of 1893, a similar reaction against the Chicago School and Sullivan had set in. Burnham's Selfridge Building of 1909 in London illustrates this tendency at its worst.

The contention that the sudden fall in the European importance of English architecture really took place shortly after 1900 is also confirmed by the development of town planning. In the planning of estates, especially garden estates, called garden cities or garden suburbs, England was ahead during the second half of the nineteenth century. From the forties the beginnings of modern planning of apartments and small houses for workmen can be traced.[21] The first planned estates of small houses were due to progressive manufacturers (Saltaire, Sir Titus Salt, begun in 1851).[22] The earliest estate of friendly, semi-detached brick houses embedded in trees was erected at Bedford Park near London to Norman Shaw's designs from 1875 onwards. Shortly after Bedford Park, Port Sunlight and Bournville were started, both garden estates for members of the staff of a big firm. Port Sunlight was built for Lever's from 1888 on, Bournville for Cadbury's from 1895 on.

The idea of the independent garden city was put forward by Ebenezer Howard in his famous book *Tomorrow: a Peaceful Path to Real Reform* (1898). It was taken up by the founders of Letchworth. The plan of this garden city (begun in 1904) was due to R. Unwin and B. Parker. The same architects were responsible for the layout of the Hampstead Garden Suburb (1907).

These English estates strongly influenced the Continent. Krupp's started its first workers' estate in 1891. The first independent garden city in Germany, Hellerau, near Dresden, was

90. Mackintosh: Cranston Tearoom, Buchanan Street, Glasgow. 1897–98

begun in 1909, by the initiative of the *Deutsche Werkstätten*. However, in Germany the main interest soon shifted over from the question of the estate of small houses to that of large schemes of tenement houses. It is this problem and the related one of planning whole suburban areas that occupied the minds of German town planners between 1900 and the war.

The history of town planning from 1850 to 1914 runs strikingly parallel to that of contemporary architecture and decoration. Of the two biggest tasks that were put to architects during the third quarter of the century, the Viennese *Ringstrasse* is a gorgeous chain of individual buildings entirely or almost entirely unrelated to each other, whereas Haussmann's memorable opening up of large boulevards all through the center of Paris is certainly much more architectural in that spatial values are not neglected for those of volume. However, in Paris as well as in Vienna, the social questions of slum clearance and rehousing remained untouched, and the same may be said of all town planning in other European and American cities. Neither did the new tendencies which started about 1890 help to solve these urgent problems. Burnham in Chicago began the movement for the erection of monumental Civic

91. Mackintosh: Dining room for the house of a connoisseur. 1901

Centers in the United States, a movement that conquered England after 1900. In Germany, Camillo Sitte's book *Der Städtebau* (1889) pleaded against the hollow grandeur of Neo-Baroque squares and roads, and proposed a freer, more picturesque planning on medieval lines. Both Sitte and Burnham still thought in terms of individual pieces of planned development.

It has been shown that the interpretation of town planning not only as a display of civic power but as planning for the welfare and comfort of the whole population originated in England and remained confined to England for well over a decade. But, as soon as planning was applied to areas larger than the garden estate of a firm, municipal initiative had to replace private enterprise. It is extremely characteristic that directly this stage was reached, England dropped out and Germany took the lead. Most German towns own a great deal of the building land within their boundaries and — helped by legislation — try to acquire more. Theodor Fischer, one of the most energetic young architects, was elected city architect for Munich in the nineties; the periodical *Der Städtebau* began to appear in 1904; towns such as Nürnberg, Ulm, Mannheim, Frankfort, worked out comprehensive schemes for the development of center and suburbs. The town-planning exhibition held at Berlin in 1910 can be taken as the final summing up of these tendencies as they flourished before the war.[23]

Since 1918, the huge housing estates set up above all in Holland, Germany and Austria have done more than any other type of building to draw the attention of other countries to the existence of a modern architectural style. In England it was hardly before 1925, or even 1930, that the public began to take any interest in the modern problem of the working-class apartment house. About the same time, the forms of the Modern Movement began to penetrate into England, the forms which, between 1900 and 1925, had been developed by American, French and German architects.

7

The Modern Movement before Nineteen-fourteen

The most progressive countries in the fifteen years before the First World War were the United States. France, Germany and Austria. At first, America took the lead; but no accepted style was evolved. The initiative was confined to a few great architects, one might even say to one man. In France, one side of the coming style was developed with admirable consistency, but again only by one group of engineer-architects. Germany alone, and those Central European countries which were dependent on Germany (Switzerland, Austria, Scandinavia) responded so appreciatively to the adventurous achievements of the first pioneers that an accepted style of our age emerged from their individual experiments.

The contribution of France to the Modern Movement before the war consists exclusively in the work of two architects: Auguste Perret and Tony Garnier. Perret was born in 1874, Garnier in 1869 (he died in 1948).[1] Their foremost distinction is that they were the first to use concrete outside and inside their buildings without concealing the material and its particular character and without adapting it to the spirit of past styles. In this, they went beyond Baudot, whose forms at St. Jean de Montmartre, though not actually copied from Gothic architecture, tend to express through the medium of concrete the feelings enshrined in the medieval cathedral. In Perret's work, there is no such irresolution. The apartment house at No. 25 bis rue Franklin, which he built in 1902–03, and in which he lives himself, is equally uncompromising in ground plan and façade (pl. 92). It is eight stories high and constructed with a concrete framework. The two uppermost floors recede in the manner which has now become compulsory in high American buildings, and is becoming more and more popular in Europe too. On top is an open terrace with a few plants, a forecast of roof gardens to come. The façade exhibits the structure to a degree unprecedented in domestic architecture. The eye is led to follow the vertical and horizontal girders and beams all along the front. A nakedness appears that seemed shameless at the time when the house was built, but seems to us to be a confession of the naked truth and therefore admirable. Equally important for future development is the expressiveness of advance and recession, the fullness of spatial effects. It is hardly possible to decide which of the various vertical planes may be termed the façade proper. Above the two entrance doors a column of square bay windows is projected. Six stories thus seem balanced without any support. In the center part, the façade recedes, but right in the middle another row of bay windows projects slightly. Mackintosh alone of all European architects had a spatial imagination of comparable brilliance. Only rarely, between 1903 and now, has Perret been so completely uncompromising as here. As a

92. Perret: Apartment house, 25 bis rue Franklin, Paris. 1902–03

rule he tends to treat concrete in a rather more playful way following, no doubt, the example set by Anatole de Baudot. This is for instance evident in his next building after the house in rue Franklin, the garage in rue Ponthieu, erected in 1905. Again the concrete frame is frankly visible. But the centerpiece of the façade is a kind of cathedral rose window made of iron bars and glass panels; and the doors are decorated with squares and diagonal lines. It would be outside the subject of this book to go more closely into the qualities of Perret's concrete ornament. It is sufficient to say that, from the very beginning, it was all but limited to rectangular forms similar to those which we have seen in England since the days of Voysey's and Gimson's beginnings.

Equally revolutionary is the style of Tony Garnier's plans for an Industrial City, begun in 1901 and exhibited in 1904.[2] Garnier (1869–1948) was a *Pensionnaire de l'Académie Française* in Rome, when he embarked upon the task of mapping out a modern city as it ought to be. *Académie Française* and Industrial City: no more dramatic contrast could be found to illustrate the difference between official architecture and the ideas of the *avant-garde* in France, a difference which, even today, prevents the new style from becoming as

93. Garnier: Industrial City. 1901–04. Administration Building

94. Garnier: Industrial City. 1901–04. Hospital

popular there as in Central Europe, Scandinavia and Holland. Though Garnier too did not abandon decoration altogether, his attitude was truly contemporary. He pleaded for a linear as against a concentric plan for his town, for a sensible grouping of industry, administration and housing, and for sufficient open spaces; he enjoyed flat roofs, open and covered playgrounds for schools, and he refused to admit any narrow inner courts. Moreover there are certain buildings in the Industrial City which appear to be wholly of today. For the first time here the possibility of "misdating" arises. In the Administration Building (pl. 93), the flat roofs, the complete absence of moldings, the contrast between the massive center block and the two sides of the façade which consist of concrete beams and glass only, and above all the covered platform on the right with its few supports — all this seems hardly possible at such an early date. Again in the long low hospital building with sun balconies to all rooms on both floors (pl. 94), the cubist disposition of blocks and slabs in the groups of private houses and the individual houses (pl. 95), the informal pathways between the houses and the old trees forming pleasant irregular patterns (pl. 96), the glass

III

95 and 96. Garnier: Industrial City.
1901–04. Houses

97. Garnier: Industrial City. 1901–04.
Palm court in a private house

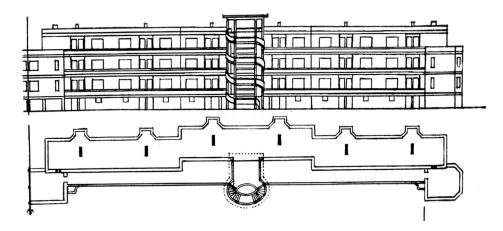

98. Garnier: Industrial City. 1901–04. Detail from a one-room apartment house

and concrete roof of a palm court in a large private house (pl. 97), are amazingly similar to the most up-to-date work after the First World War. There are in one block of single-room apartments even two open spiral staircases (above) exposed to the outside in such a way that one remains in doubt whether this points back to François I at Blois or forward to Gropius.

Garnier's later work is a little more conventional in detail, a typically French quality. For France has always, after a short time, made her own brilliant revolutions conform to legitimate tradition.

Le Corbusier[3] (born in 1887) is not a Frenchman. He comes from the French-speaking part of Switzerland, the puritan part which gave birth to Calvin and still gives birth to the world's best watchmakers. This is probably what made him resist the temptation of French rhetoric and keep to an equally French logic and dry grace. However, Le Corbusier scarcely belongs to a book dealing with pre-war matters; though he has tried in his writings to make himself appear one of the pioneers, he was not among the first comers. His designs for an estate called *Domino,* which was to be built entirely in concrete, are certainly very progressive; but they date from 1915, and in 1916 Le Corbusier could still build a private house that does not go beyond the stage reached by Perret or van de Velde before the war.[4] The historian must emphasize this point, because Le Corbusier, partly owing to his magnificent artistic imagination and partly to a certain showmanship, has been taken for one of the creators of the Modern Movement.

It is surprising how, after so short a time as twenty or thirty years, historical facts already tend to become dim and legends begin to grow up. The historian of art will find the same if he goes into the beginnings of Cubism in French painting, or Expressionism in German painting. Who created Cubism? Picasso or Braque? When was the *Brücke* founded? What part, in establishing the style of that group, was played by Heckel, Kirchner, Pechstein, or even Nolde?[5] There are many similar questions.

Turn to the United States, and you will find no such obscure patches. Research carried out more consistently and tenaciously than anywhere else has cleared up the dates and

99. Sullivan and Wright: Charnley house, Chicago. 1891

vicissitudes of the American pioneers of the Modern Movement — which means, broadly speaking, Sullivan and Frank Lloyd Wright. Of Sullivan much has already been said regarding his revolutionary theory (p. 13), his revolutionary ornament (p. 58) and his revolutionary treatment of the skyscraper in its earlier years (p. 82). His most astonishing esthetic achievement however is the Schlesinger & Mayer, now Carson Pirie Scott Store in Chicago (pl. 100). This was begun in 1899 on Madison Street and enlarged by a taller block around the corner into State Street in 1903–04. The ornament on the ground floor and second floor is Sullivan at his most brilliant and fanciful, but the upper stories exhibit the rhythm of the twentieth century more uncompromisingly than any building we have met so far in these pages. Here again, a detail photograph of several rows of these horizontal windows with the unbroken white bands which separate them horizontally would no doubt be misdated by nearly everybody.

Meanwhile, Frank Lloyd Wright had begun to revolutionize the private house with similar courage.[6] His inspiration came from Richardson's houses and from the forms and approach to architecture which he learned in Sullivan's office. The Charnley house on Astor Street, Chicago, of 1891 (above), seems both to reflect Sullivan's style in the Wainwright Building and to foretell Wright's own later development. It can therefore be safely assumed that it represents Wright's fairly independent designing during the years when he was still employed by Sullivan. In date and originality it corresponds to Voysey's houses in Hans Road.

Two years later the Winslow house at River Forest (pl. 101) has the same sense of broad flat surfaces and the same consistent emphasis on horizontals. It still possesses an upper floor decorated in the Sullivan manner and nothing yet of Wright's future mastery of spatial planning. Compared with Voysey at Colwall in the same year 1893, it is clear that

100. Sullivan: Carson Pirie Scott Store, Chicago. 1899 and 1903–04

Wright was moving away from precedent, Voysey towards a synthesis between the past and the present.

Wright's sense of three-dimensional composition leaped to maturity about 1900. The projected Yahara Boat Club at Madison of 1902 (pl. 103) shows far projecting canopies over the two doors and far stretching-out terraces in front of them, taking some outer space close to the body of a house which is however still strictly symmetrical in its shape. The windows, high up and low, are now entirely of the characteristic rhythm of the Modern Movement.

Another three years and the W. R. Heath house at Buffalo (pl. 102) has a plan spreading out loosely into a conglomeration of rooms which run comfortably into each other, and an outline of the broad, free, informal, Prairie type of which Wright is so fond. There is no

101. Wright: Winslow house, River Forest, Illinois. 1893

102. Wright: Heath house, Buffalo, New York. 1905

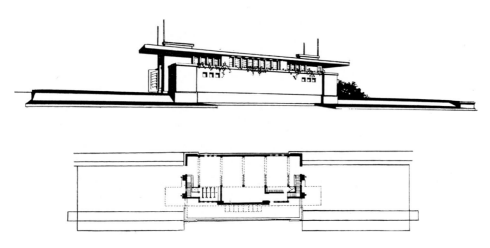

103. Wright: Project for the Yahara Boat Club, Madison, Wisconsin. 1902

116

104. Wright: Coonley house, Riverside, Illinois. 1908. Interior

longer any hard boundary between outer and inner space. The low spacious interiors (above) have something irresistibly inviting, in spite of Wright's never abating desire for harsh angular decorative forms — forms similar to those of Berlage in Europe. No wonder that the Dutch were the first to take kindly to Wright's peculiar style when it had been made known abroad by two German publications of 1910 and 1911.[7]

The same difference between early and mature as that between the Winslow and Heath houses is to be found between a design for a skyscraper done in 1895 and the Larkin Building at Buffalo of 1904 (pls. 106 and 105). The skyscraper is again a personal paraphrase of Sullivan ideas, the Larkin Building, with its sheer walls of flat bricks unrelieved by windows or niches or moldings, and with its string courses and cornices of the simplest rectangular profile, is overwhelmingly impressive, in the hard-hitting ruthless way of today. The interior with its spatial unity of all floors (pl. 107), the "etherealization" of which Wright is so fond (see p. 14) may be derived from the European department store. In Wright's particular form it became the prototype of many similar halls in European office buildings after the First World War.

To sum up, Frank Lloyd Wright's outstanding importance lies in the fact that nobody else had by 1904 come so near to the style of today in his actual buildings. Wright's later activity does not lie within the scope of this book, and, as the work of his followers before 1914 has not added anything essential beyond the master's own pronouncements, no more need be said here about the United States.

Thus the remaining pages can be devoted exclusively to Germany and Austria.[8] While the transition to the new simplicity and severity was facilitated in England by the absence of *Art Nouveau* and by an inborn English reasonableness, in America by the technical requirements of the huge office building, and in France by the splendid traditions of nine-

117

105. Wright: Larkin Building, Buffalo, New York. 1904

teenth-century engineering, Germany was, in 1900, almost completely under the spell of *Art Nouveau,* enjoying wild ornamentation, as she had done so often in past centuries. Only a few among those who had played a leading part in the *Jugendstil* found a way out of its entanglement. Two artists above all must be mentioned, as a German parallel to Mackintosh in Great Britain.

August Endell's (1871–1925) most popular work was the Elvira Studio in Munich, built for a photographer in 1897–98 (pl. 108). The deliberate lack of balance between openings and plain wall, or basement windows and ground-floor windows, and also the curves of the metal bars separating the window panes, were not unlike early Mackintosh. However, the one dominant motif of the façade, that overpowering shape, shell-like or dragon-like, which covered the wall of the second floor, was entirely opposed to Mackintosh's delicate handwriting. In this frantic outbreak of ornamental fury, the unbounded exuberance of German patterns of the migration period re-emerged. This eternal quality of German art, traceable in Late Romanesque and Late Gothic as well as in the ornament of Baroque and Rococo, gave Endell his place in architecture; though it seems highly probable that Obrist's embroideries provided him with more direct inspiration. Be that as it may, the Elvira Studio remains an admirable *tour de force,* and one could rightly expect more surprises from its inventor.

In the same year, when the front of the studio building was unveiled, Endell published a study on the emotional meaning of certain basic proportions in building which is equally original and inspiring.[9] The text to the illustration shown here (pl. 109) describes the quiet balance of *fig. 4*, the strain of *fig. 2*, a certain ease and comfortableness in *fig. 3*. Apart from this interesting attempt at an interpretation of architecture as an abstract art, the forms of the façade shown in *fig. 3* are astonishingly similar to those of certain German houses after the First World War. The shape of the second-floor windows and the flat roof are again almost "misdatable."

A similar originality within *Art Nouveau* appears in the works of Josef Maria Olbrich (1867–1908).[10] Together with the painter Klimt, Olbrich was amongst the founders of the *Sezession* in Vienna, the group that developed the Austrian version of *Art Nouveau*, and later on led the way from linear decoration towards the more architectural though equally graceful style of the *Wiener Werkstätte*. The building of the *Sezession* (pl. 110) was designed and erected by Olbrich in 1898–99. There is no need here to say much about the *Jugendstil* qualities of this metal cupola with its superabundant floral decoration. A more essential point in our context is the simplicity of its semicircular contour and the rhythm of the three blocks which dominate the front view. This is in fact as novel as anything to be found in Wright's work of the same period.[11] In 1907–08, Olbrich built the *Hochzeitsturm* (pl. 111) as a center of the artists' colony which the Grand Duke of Hessen had started in 1899 (cf. p. 140). Again a comparison with Mackintosh, this time with the

106. Wright: Design for a skyscraper. 1895

107. Wright: Larkin Building, Buffalo, New York. 1904. Interior

108. Endell: Elvira Studio, Munich. 1897–98

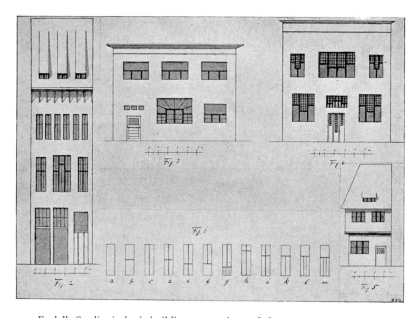

109. Endell: Studies in basic building proportions. 1898

library wing of the Glasgow Art School, seems justified. The conspicuous five organ-pipe like shapes on top of the tower are characteristic of the restlessness of many of those who wanted to break away from *Art Nouveau,* but felt unable to make an altogether fresh start.

110. Olbrich: The *Sezession*, Vienna. 1898–99

The most remarkable feature from the point of view of today is the two narrow horizontal strips with small windows which are wrapped around the corner, the earliest instance probably of this motif, so much favored by later architects.

In reviewing the work of the second leader of Viennese architecture at the beginning of the twentieth century, we are led one step farther. The most remarkable of Josef Hoffmann's (born in 1870)[12] early works is the Stoclet house in Brussels (pl. 112), designed in 1905. Its unusual size and splendor have overshadowed other works of Hoffmann's that are even more important in the evolution of the modern style. No doubt the Palais Stoclet is a work of exceedingly spirited composition, its exquisitely spaced openings and light walls are a joy to the eye, and the high uninterrupted window of the staircase has become a very popular motif since about 1920; but the artistic attitude is far from *sachlich* (rightly, no doubt): a charm and playfulness are expressed in these façades which are alien to most of the outstanding buildings after 1914, though they are essentially Austrian in character. In acknowledging the international unity of the new style, it ought not to be forgotten that in Hoffmann's elegance, in Perret's clarity, in Wright's expansive broadness and comfortable solidity, or in Gropius' uncompromising directness, national qualities are represented at their best. The Austrian character of Hoffmann's art remains in full, even in his simplest

111. Olbrich: *Hochzeitsturm*, Darmstadt. 1907

112. Hoffmann: Palais Stoclet, Brussels. 1905

and most "modern" work, the Convalescent Home in Purkersdorf, 1903–04 (pl. 113).
Here again, even experts might be deceived and might take these flat roofs, these windows
without any moldings, the squareness of this projecting roof over the entrance, and the
high, upright staircase window as something impossible before the First World War. Inter-

113. Hoffmann: Convalescent Home, Purkersdorf. 1903–04

national as these motifs are, local peculiarities are clearly visible in the rhythm of the small windowpanes and the delicate bands running around the windows and along the edges of the block.

But the art historian has to watch personal as well as national qualities. Only the interaction of these with an age produces the complete picture of the art of an epoch, as we see it. Rubens, Bernini, Rembrandt, Vermeer are all representatives of their age, the age of Baroque. Yet Rubens is as wholly a Fleming as Bernini is a Neapolitan, and Rembrandt and Vermeer are Dutchmen. But Rembrandt as a personality is completely opposed to Vermeer, when one compares them within the smaller orbit of their national art. So it may be profitable to contrast Hoffmann's delightful building with the work of Adolf Loos[13] (1870–1933), so completely opposed in character, though Loos was also an Austrian. His position in the development of esthetic theory about 1900 has already been outlined. Now we have to define his place in architectural history proper. Remembering his attacks on ornament and his panegyrics upon the plumber, we are not surprised to find in his first work, the interior of a shop in Vienna, 1898 (pl. 114), nothing that can, strictly speaking, be called

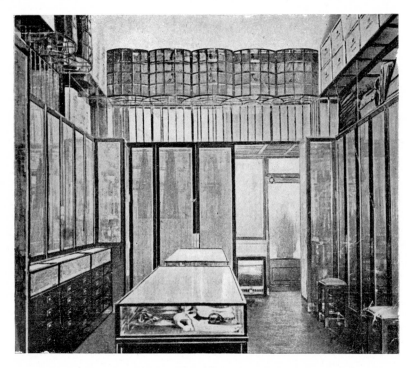

114. Loos: Shop interior, Vienna. 1898

ornament. The value of this work depends entirely on the high quality of the materials used and the dignity of the proportions. The decorative effect of the upper frieze is obtained by the introduction of convex curves and a quicker rhythm of intersecting verticals and horizontals. Perret's concrete ornament, created without any knowledge of Loos's style, is surprisingly similar in character.

Six years later, in a house on Lake Geneva (pl. 115) Loos reached the same delicately proportioned simplicity in an exterior, and another six years after that, in the Steiner house in Vienna (pl. 116), he achieved the style of today completely and without any limitation. The unmitigated contrast of receding center and projecting wings, the unbroken line of the roofs, the small openings in the attic, the horizontal windows with their large undivided panes: who, without being informed, would not date this house about 1924–30, or even later?[14] Loos is one of the greatest creators in modern architecture. In spite of that, he never became known, during his lifetime, to more than a small circle of admirers. His influence remained negligible for a long time. All the other pioneers were more widely discussed and imitated.

Among German architects, Peter Behrens[15] (born in 1868) was probably the most important of those responsible for the diffusion of the new style. Like so many other leading German architects after 1900, he began as a painter and underwent the ''moral'' reformation towards the applied arts, before he trained as an architect. The applied arts, when Behrens started, meant *Art Nouveau*. He soon escaped from this enervating atmosphere. His first building, his own house in Darmstadt (1901), already shows a hardening of the tender

115. Loos: Private house on Lake Geneva. 1904

116. Loos: Steiner house, Vienna. 1910

curves of *Art Nouveau*.[16] A year later, Behrens designed a type face in which the change is complete. The curves are straightened, and ornamental initials are decorated with squares and circles only. A comparison between Behrens' first type faces and Eckmann's (1900) is historically very instructive.[17] Again this new simplicity was brought about under English

117. Schröder: Apartment for A. W. von Heymel, Berlin. 1901

influence. The Doves Press stands at the beginning of German twentieth-century printing. Honesty, health and straightforwardness became the ideals that replaced the sultry dreams of *Art Nouveau* esthetes.

Behrens was not alone in this revulsion from *Art Nouveau*. Its earliest witness in Germany seems to be the apartment designed by R. A. Schröder (born 1878), a poet and decorator and one of the founders of the Insel Verlag, for Alfred Walter von Heymel (1878–1914), also a poet and also a founder of the Insel Verlag. The apartment was in Berlin and dates from 1901 (above).[18] Here for the first time — even if perhaps not without some inspiration from the hieratic stiffness of some Mackintosh furniture — are chairs without curves, and walls, ceilings and fireplaces divided into simple rectangular geometric patterns.

In Behrens' buildings from 1904 onwards the same new somewhat classicist spirit is expressed in the exteriors. Take for instance the Art Building at an exhibition held at Oldenburg in 1905 (pl. 118) and compare it with Olbrich's *Sezession*. In Behrens' building the florid cupola and the curved cornice have disappeared. The centerpiece and the outer pavilions have roofs of pyramidal form — a motif derived from Olbrich's Exhibition Building in Darmstadt, 1901 (pl. 111 on the right) — the rest of the building has flat roofs. Walls without windows are decorated with delicate lines forming oblong panels and squares. The porch has been left completely bare, just two square posts and a square lintel.

This indicates the direction in which Behrens was to develop during the years that followed. His principal buildings before the war he designed for the AEG, one of the big German electrical combines, of which the managing director, P. Jordan, had appointed him architect and adviser. In 1909 the turbine factory was built, perhaps the most beautiful industrial building ever erected up to that time (pl. 119). The steel frame is clearly exhibited, wide, perfectly spaced glass panes replace the walls on the side, while at the corners stone is used to emphasize the weight and strength of the colossal pile. This design has

118. Behrens: Art Building, Oldenburg Exhibition. 1905

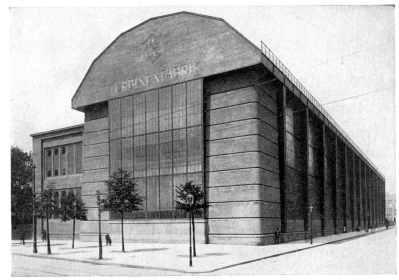

119. Behrens: Turbine factory, Huttenstrasse, Berlin. 1909

120. Behrens: Factory, Volta-strasse, Berlin. 1911

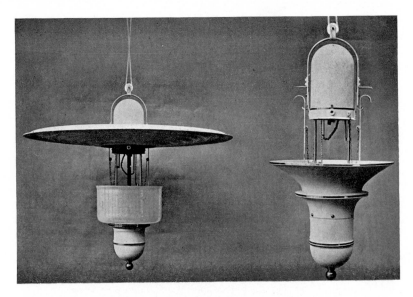

121. Behrens: Street lamps for the AEG. 1907–08

122. Ehmcke: Basket and box in silver. 1907

nothing in common with the ordinary factory of that time. Even more clearly than in American grain-elevators, the imaginative possibilities of industrial architecture are visualized. The result is a pure work of art, so finely balanced that the huge dimensions are scarcely realized, unless one looks at the people in the street for comparison. The two-storied aisle on the left has the flat roof and the row of windows which we find in all the most advanced works of that time.

The factory for the production of small electric motors was built in 1911 (pl. 120). The

123. Paul and the *Deutsche Werkstätten:* Dining room. 1906

proportions of that part of the building which is to be seen on the left, its rows of rather narrow high windows without any moldings, are reminiscent of the factory of 1909 and very different from Hoffmann's or Loos's or Gropius' favorite proportions. The same strength and noble vigor are expressed in the composition of the main block with its round-fronted pillars and recessed windows. However, it would be wrong to assume that Behrens' style fitted only the severe world of industry. One of the best buildings erected in the years before the First World War for the purpose of representing national grandeur was also designed by him: the German Embassy in St. Petersburg (1913).

It is all the more admirable that the artist, while he was employed on such monumental tasks, spent the same amount of care and thought on improvements in the design of machine-made industrial products which had never before been regarded as works of art at all. It may well be that future history will set as much store by these small works as by his big buildings. Only two instances can be given here, two street lamps for the AEG (pl. 121). They show the same purity of form, the same sobriety in limiting the design to simple geometrical forms, and the same beauty of proportion which delight us in Behrens' buildings.

129

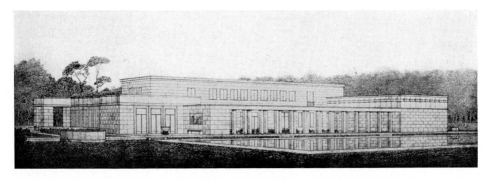

124. Mies van der Rohe: Project for the Kröller house. 1912

The *Deutscher Werkbund* was founded in 1907. Of its successful propaganda for high standards of craftsmanship and industrial design, something has been said in Chapter 1. To give an idea of its actual work, one illustration must suffice. The silver basket and silver box in plate 122 were designed in 1907 by E. H. Ehmcke, who is best known as one of the foremost German book designers. The two silver objects are not handmade; they were produced in a factory by means of machinery — and, as their shapes clearly express this, their esthetic value is not at all affected.

The same applies to the furniture designed by Bruno Paul[19] (born in 1874) for the *Deutsche Werkstätten*. We have already mentioned that Paul was the designer of the first modern "unit" furniture which came out in 1910,[20] and that he and the founder of the *Deutsche Werkstätten* worked out the first quantity-produced and machine-produced furniture of modern design. That was in 1906. The dining room shown in plate 123 was exhibited in Dresden in that year. Again we see a personal taste utterly different from the Viennese as well as from Behrens'. Paul and the *Deutsche Werkstätten* do not mind a touch of tradition; they dislike principles of inhuman rigidity; comfort, cleanliness and the abolition of tawdry fuss is all they desire. This attitude enabled them to popularize the new style in Germany. Bruno Paul and Karl Schmidt were not revolutionary; nor was the *Werkbund*. This explains why they were able to effect a change of taste throughout the country, which Gropius, the most uncompromising German innovator, might not have been able to bring about.

Before passing on to Gropius' work, a few words must be said about some early buildings by one or two other German architects. Ludwig Mies van der Rohe[21] was born in 1886, Hans Poelzig[22] in 1869 (he died in 1936). They represent two opposite possibilities of self-expression in terms of the new style. Mies van der Rohe's design for the Kröller house of 1912 (above) is evidently derived from Behrens, but also, though perhaps less evidently, from Schinkel, the great Prussian architect of the Classical Revival who was just then being rediscovered and reappreciated.[23] From him come Mies's sparseness and extreme precision, from him and Behrens his sense of cubic relations.

Mies's Kröller house has a permanence even in the drawing and a convincing monumentality which makes Poelzig's office building in Breslau of 1911 (pl. 125) look as if it

125. Poelzig: Office building, Breslau. 1911

were surging ponderously towards us. These thick bands curving around the corner, which have by now become almost a matter of course with office buildings in cities, are of great dynamic power, in spite of their somewhat elephantine detail. Much more sensitive is Poelzig's chemical factory in Luban of 1911–12 (pl. 126) with its general attitude of *Sachlichkeit,* its free grouping of blocks, and its oddly spaced and shaped windows.

The end of this survey is reached now that we have arrived at the work of Walter Gropius (born in 1883). His first buildings mark the fulfillment of the style of our century; entirely representative of the spirit of today, they hide their real dates more effectively than anything we have yet seen, except Loos's villa of 1910. Gropius worked for some time in Peter Behrens' studio (1907–10). Soon after that, in 1911, he was commissioned to build a factory at Alfeld on the Leine (*Faguswerk,* pls. 128, 129). His designs go distinctly beyond those by Behrens for the AEG. Only small details such as the windows in the foreground of plate 128 and on the right of the main block in plate 129 show Behrens' influence. As for the main block itself, everything is new and full of stimulating ideas. For the first time a complete façade is conceived in glass. The supporting piers are reduced to narrow bands of steel. The corners are left without any support, a treatment which has since been imitated over and over again. The expression of the flat roof has also changed. Only in the building by Loos which was done one year before the Fagus Factory, have we seen the same feeling for the pure cube. Behrens' composed balance between verticals and horizontals has been abandoned; an advancing horizontal movement of great energy, here dominates the composition.

131

126. Poelzig: Chemical factory, Luban. 1911–12

127. Gropius and Meyer: Model factory, Werkbund Exhibition, Cologne. 1914.
North side

Another exceedingly important quality of Gropius' building is that, thanks to the new treatment of glass and steel, the usual hard separation of exterior and interior is annihilated. Light and air can pass freely through the walls so that the closed-in space is no longer different in essence from the great universe of space outside. This "etherealization" of architecture, as Frank Lloyd Wright had called it in 1901,[24] is one of the most characteristic features of the new style; and it may be the highest artistic merit of nineteenth-century engineers that they were the first to aspire to it. It has been shown that a never satisfied ambition led them to bridge ever larger spaces with steel and concrete and to reduce the weight of the walls and the weight of the ceilings to the utmost, until the cupola of the *Jahrhunderthalle* at Breslau, designed by the architect Max Berg in 1910–12, covered an area of 20,800 square feet in concrete with a weight of only 4200 tons (cupola of St. Peter's, Rome: 5249 square feet, weight *c.* 10,000 tons).

This same longing for weightlessness and flexibility, we have found in the usual ground plan of nineteenth-century office buildings, where the supporting steel girders made all the partition walls easily removable. We have seen it again in Wright's ground plans of private

128 and 129. Gropius and Meyer: Fagus Factory, Alfeld on the Leine. 1911

130. Gropius and Meyer: Model factory, Werkbund Exhibition, Cologne. 1914.
South side

houses, in the arrangement of the rooms in Perret's house of 1903, in Mackintosh's en-
trancing vistas; and we may also recognize it in the sweeping plans for the future layout of
whole provinces, which were first made in Germany immediately after the First World War
(*Landesplanung,* Ruhr District, 1920). Here too it is the conquest of space, the spanning
of great distances, the rational co-ordination of heterogeneous functions that fascinates
architects. The profound affinity of this modern enthusiasm for *planning* (architectural as
well as political) with the style of Gropius' Fagus Factory is evident. The forms of the
building reveal the mind of an artist but also of a sagacious thinker. Calculation and vision
have worked together, as they did in the days of the cathedral builders, of Brunelleschi,
Alberti and Michelangelo. The warm and direct feelings of the great men of the past may

have gone; but then the artist who is representative of this century of ours must needs be cold, as he stands for a century cold as steel and glass, a century the precision of which leaves less space for self-expression than did any period before.

However, the great creative brain will find its own way even in times of overpowering collective energy, even with the medium of this new style of the twentieth century which, because it is a genuine style as opposed to a passing fashion, is universal. For the Werkbund Exhibition of 1914, Gropius built a small model factory (pl. 127). The north side is his comment on his master's turbine factory of five years before. The reduction of motifs to an absolute minimum and the sweeping simplification of outline are patent. The replacement of Behrens' heavy corner piers by thin metallic lines should be specially noted. Bolder still is the south front with the superb contrast between the massive brick center and the completely glazed corners (pl. 130). In the middle there are only the narrowest slits for the windows and the lowest Wrightian entrance; at the corner, where according to all standards of the past, a sufficient-looking supporting force should show itself, there is nothing but glass encasing transparently two spiral staircases.

The motif has since been imitated as often as the girderless corner of the Fagus Factory; and it shows that Gropius' personal expression is by no means lacking in grace. There is something sublime in this effortless mastery of material and weight. Never since the Sainte-Chapelle and the choir of Beauvais had the human art of building been so triumphant over matter. Yet the character of the new buildings is entirely un-Gothic, anti-Gothic. While in the thirteenth century all lines, functional though they were, served the one artistic purpose of pointing heavenwards to a goal beyond this world, and walls were made translucent to carry the transcendental magic of saintly figures rendered in colored glass, the glass walls are now clear and without mystery, the steel frame is hard, and its expression discourages all other-worldly speculation. It is the creative energy of this world in which we live and work and which we want to master, a world of science and technique, of speed and danger, of hard struggles and no personal security, that is glorified in Gropius' architecture.

Notes

1. Theories of Art from Morris to Gropius

1. John Ruskin, *Architecture and Painting,* 1853. Addenda to Lectures I and II, Library Edition, vol. xii, 1904, p. 83 and *The Seven Lamps of Architecture,* New York, 1849, p. 7; Sir George Gilbert Scott, *Remarks on Secular and Domestic Architecture,* London, 1858, p. 221.

2. Sir George Gilbert Scott, *Personal and Professional Recollections,* London, 1879, p. 117 ff.

3. Cf. J. W. Mackail, *The Life of William Morris,* London, 1899. On Morris' place in the history of 19th century theories of art, cf. Nikolaus Pevsner, "Gemeinschaftsideale unter den bildenden Künstlern des 19. Jahrhunderts," *Deutsche Vierteljahrsschrift für Literaturwissenschaft und Geistesgeschichte,* ix, 1931, p. 143 ff. On Morris' importance for the 20th century see Nikolaus Pevsner, "William Morris, C. R. Ashbee und das zwanzigste Jahrhundert," *Deutsche Vierteljahrsschrift für Literaturwissenschaft und Geistesgeschichte,* xiv, 1936, p. 536 ff.

4. Mackail, *op. cit.,* ii, p. 80.

5. *The Collected Works of William Morris,* London, 1915, xxiii, p. 147.

6. *Ibid.,* 1914, xxii, p. 26.

7. Mackail, *op. cit.,* ii, p. 99.

8. *Coll. Works of William Morris,* xxii, p. 42; xxiii, p. 173.

9. *Ibid.,* xxii, pp. 47, 50, 58, 73, 80, etc.

10. Mackail, *op. cit.,* i, p. 186.

11. *Coll. Works of William Morris,* xxii, p. 47.

12. Mackail, *op. cit.,* ii, p. 106.

13. *Coll. Works of William Morris,* xxiii, pp. 194, 201.

14. Mackail, *op. cit.,* ii, p. 105.

15. *Ibid.,* p. 144; i, p. 305.

16. *Coll. Works of William Morris,* xxii, p. 75.

17. W. R. Lethaby, *Philip Webb and His Work,* Oxford, 1935, p. 94. One of the first to notice this contradiction was Morris' earliest French follower, Henri Cazalis (1840–1909), who wrote under the pseudonym Jean Lahor. Cf. his *W. Morris et le mouvement nouveau de l'art décoratif,* Geneva, 1897, p. 41–42; also T. Walton, "A French disciple of William Morris 'Jean Lahor,'" *Revue de littérature comparée,* 1935, pp. 524–535.

18. *Coll. Works of William Morris,* xxii, pp. 335–336.

19. *Ibid.,* pp. 352, 336; xxiii, p. 179.

20. Arts and Crafts Exhibition Society, *Catalogue I,* London, 1888, p. 7.

21. The National Association for the Advancement of Art and its Application to Industry, *Transactions, Liverpool Meeting, 1888,* London, 1888, p. 216.

22. Walter Crane, *The Claims of Decorative Art,* Boston, 1892, p. 75.

23. Arts and Crafts Exhibition Society, *Catalogue III,* London, 1890, p. 8.

24. Crane, *op. cit.,* p. 6.

25. *Ibid.,* pp. 76, 65.

26. Cf. Pevsner, *Deutsche Vierteljahrsschrift . . .,* xiv, 1936.

27. Charles R. Ashbee, *A Few Chapters on Workshop Reconstruction and Citizenship,* London, 1894, pp. 16, 24.

28. *Idem, An Endeavour towards the Teachings of J. Ruskin and W. Morris* [London, 1901] p. 47.

29. *Idem, Craftsmanship in Competitive Industry* [Campden, Glos., 1908] p. 194.

30. *Idem, Should We Stop Teaching Art?* London [1911] p. 4; *Where the Great City Stands,* London, 1917, p. 3.

31. Lewis F. Day, *Everyday Art: Short Essays on the Arts Not-Fine,* London, 1882, pp. 273–274.

32. John D. Sedding, *Art and Handicraft,* London, 1893, pp. 128–129.

33. Above all Lethaby; cf. his lectures on Modern German Architecture and on Design and Industry, delivered in 1915: "Up to twenty years ago there had been a very remarkable development of English art in all kinds . . . Then . . . there came a timid reaction and the re-emergence of the catalogued 'styles' . . . German advances . . . have been founded on the English Arts and Crafts. They saw the essence of our best essays in furniture, glass, textiles, printing, and all the rest . . ." *Form in Civilisation,* London, 1922, p. 46 ff. and 96 ff. Cf. also Ashbee who, in his *Should We Stop Teaching Art?,* p. 4, says that since about 1900 the growth of the English movement "has been arrested, and its principles are now more consistently and logically studied in Germany and America."

34. Oscar Wilde, *Essays and Lectures,* 4th ed., London, 1913, p. 178.

35. Otto Wagner, *Moderne Architektur,* Vienna, 1896, p. 95.

36. Adolf Loos, *Ins Leere gesprochen, 1897–1900,* Innsbruck, 1932, p. 18.

37. Henri van de Velde, *Die Renaissance im modernen Kunstgewerbe,* Berlin, 1901, p. 23.

38. Louis Sullivan, *Kindergarten Chats,* New York, 1947. They were first serialized in the *Interstate Architect and Builder,* February 8, 1901 to February 16, 1902.

39. *Ibid.,* p. 187.

40. Arts and Crafts Exhibition Society, *Catalogue II,* London, 1889, p. 7.

41. *The Studio,* i, p. 234.

42. The first of them was delivered in that adventurous club of young Belgian artists which was originally called *Les XX,* and since 1894 *La Libre esthétique.* Cf. Madeleine Octave Maus, *Trente années de lutte pour l'art, 1884–1914,* Brussels, 1926. Van de Velde's lectures are collected in two books: *Kunstgewerbliche Laienpredigten,* Leipzig [1902] and *Die Renaissance im modernen Kunstgewerbe,* Leipzig, 1903. Maus, *op. cit.,* p. 183, gives 1894 as the date of the first lecture, van de Velde 1890. The latter date seems highly improbable, because we know from van de Velde's biography that he had a nervous breakdown in 1889 and did not really recover until 1893 (Karl Ernst Osthaus, *Van de Velde,* Hagen, 1920, p. 10). Moreover, he admitted that he and his friends knew nothing of the English Arts and Crafts before 1891 (*Die Renaissance . . .,* p. 61). As early as 1901 critics complained of inaccuracies in van de Velde's historical accounts (*Dekorative Kunst,* vii, p. 376).

43. Van de Velde, *Die Renaissance . . .,* p. 98.

44. *Idem, . . . Laienpredigten,* p. 36.

45. *Idem, Die Renaissance . . .,* pp. 30, 111–112.

46. *Idem, . . . Laienpredigten,* p. 172.

47. *Idem, Die Renaissance . . .,* pp. 12, 111.

48. *Ibid.,* p. 110. This is identical with the principles of industrial art put forward by the British Design and Industries Association from its very foundation in 1915: fitness for use, and honesty towards materials and working processes.

49. *Idem, . . . Laienpredigten,* p. 166. How strikingly topical is this statement, too, if one replaces cement by concrete, and celluloid by plastics.

50. *Idem, Die Renaissance . . .,* p. 36.

51. *Ibid.,* p. 91.

52. Heinrich Kulka, *Adolf Loos: Das Werk des Architekten,* Vienna, 1931, p. 11.

53. Otto Wagner, *Moderne Architektur,* Vienna, 1896; J. A. Lux, *Otto Wagner,* Munich [1914]

54. Wagner, *op. cit.,* p. 8.

55. *Ibid.,* p. 37.

56. *Ibid.,* p. 41.

57. *Ibid.,* p. 37.

58. *Ibid.,* p. 99.

59. Loos, *op. cit.* His writings after 1900 were printed in a volume called *Trotzdem, 1900–1930,* Innsbruck, 1931.

60. *Idem, Ins Leere gesprochen,* p. 66. In 1908 Loos wrote an article called "Ornament and Crime," which was reprinted in *Trotzdem,* p. 79 ff.

61. *Idem, Ins Leere gesprochen,* p. 49.

62. *Ibid.,* p. 58.

63. *Ibid.,* p. 78.

64. Reprinted in Frank Lloyd Wright, *Modern Architecture,* Princeton, 1931, p. 7 ff.

65. *Ibid.,* p. 8.

66. *Ibid.,* p. 20.

67. *Ibid.,* p. 8.

68. *Ibid.,* p. 16.

69. *Ibid.,* p. 15.

70. *Ibid.,* p. 14.

71. *Ibid.,* p. 20.

72. Address at the First International Congress of Architects, quoted from Sigfried Giedion, *Space, Time and Architecture,* Cambridge, Mass., 1941, p. 151.

73. H. P. Berlage, "Over Architectuur," *Tweemaandelijk Tijdschrift,* ii, part 1, 1896, pp. 233–234. Dr. H. Gerson was kind enough to look up for me the exact words of Berlage's text.

74. H. P. Berlage, *Gedanken über Stil in der Baukunst,* Leipzig, 1905, p. 48.

75. Cf. many quotations in Fritz Schmalenbach, *Jugendstil,* Würzburg, 1935, a very useful book, which describes minutely the history of the decorative arts in Germany between 1895 and 1902.

76. Richard Graul, *Die Krisis im Kunstgewerbe,* Leipzig, 1901, p. 2.

77. Hermann Muthesius, "Kunst und Maschine," *Dekorative Kunst,* ix, 1901–1902, p. 141 ff.

78. *Idem, Stilarchitektur und Baukunst,* Mülheim-Ruhr, 1902, pp. 50, 51, 53.

79. Alfred Lichtwark, *Palastfenster und Flügeltür,* Berlin, 1899, pp. 128, 144, 169; *idem, Makartbouquet und Blumenstrauss,* Munich, 1894.

80. Hermann Obrist, "Neue Möglichkeiten in der bildenden Kunst," *Kunstwart,* xvi, part 2, 1903, p. 21.

81. W. Schäfer, "Die neue Kunstgewerbeschule in Düsseldorf," *Die Rheinlande,* 1903, pp. 62–63.

82. Friedrich Naumann, "Die Kunst im Zeitalter der Maschine," *Kunstwart,* xvii, part 2, 1904, p. 323.

83. Cf. J. Popp, *Die Deutschen Werkstätten,* written about 1923, typescript. I am greatly indebted to the late Karl Schmidt for kindly letting me read the typescript and lending me a series of photographs of D. W. furniture.

84. "Der Bund will eine Auslese der besten in Kunst, Industrie, Handwerk und Handel tätigen Kräfte vollziehen. Er will zusammenfassen, was in Qualitätsleistung und Streben in der gewerblichen Arbeit vorhanden ist. Er bildet den Sammelpunkt für alle, welche zur Qualitätsleistung befähigt und gewillt sind." On the history of the Werkbund cf. *Die Form,* vii, 1932, pp. 297–324.

85. *Ibid.,* p. 302.

86. *Ibid.,* p. 310.

87. *The Beginnings of a Journal of the D. I. A.,* 1916, p. 6.

88. Nikolaus Pevsner, *Academies of Art, Past and Present,* Cambridge, England, 1940, pp. 267, 281 ff.

89. *Die Form, loc. cit.,* pp. 316, 317.

90. This was never published. Letter of W. Gropius to the author, January 16, 1936.

91. Letter of W. Gropius to the author, January 16, 1936.

92. Cf. William Morris: "The synonym for applied art is architecture," National Association for the Advancement of Art and its Application to Industry, *Transactions, Edinburgh Meeting, 1889,* London, 1890, p. 192.

93. Walter Gropius, *The New Architecture and the Bauhaus,* New York, The Museum of Modern Art [1936]

94. Walter Gropius *et al., Staatliches Bauhaus in Weimar, 1919–1923,* Weimar, n.d., p. 8.

2. *From Eighteen-fifty-one to Morris and the Arts and Crafts*

1. *The Principal Speeches and Addresses of H. R. H. the Prince Consort,* London, 1862, pp. 110, 111.

2. *The Great Exhibition of the Works of Industry of All Nations, 1851,* London, 1851, introductory volume, p. 1.

3. Cf. J. L. and Barbara Hammond, *The Town Labourer. 1760–1832, the New Civilization,* London, 1917, who quote some typical sayings of members of the upper class in defending their unscrupulous attitude with the weapons of utilitarian philosophy: "Trade, industry and barter always find their own level" (Pitt). "By following the dictates of their own interests, landowners and farmers become, in the natural order of things, the best trustees and guardians for the public" (Rep. H. Comm. Poor Laws, 1827).

4. J. W. Mackail, *The Life of William Morris,* London, 1899, ii, p. 5.

5. Mackail says *(loc. cit.,* ii, p. 272): "Sir Edward Burne-Jones told me that Morris would have liked the faces in his pictures less highly finished, and less charged with the concentrated meaning or emotion of the painting. As with the artists of Greece and of the Middle Ages, the human face was to him merely a part, though no doubt a very important part, of the human body."

6. Nikolaus Pevsner, "Christopher Dresser, Industrial Designer," *The Architectural Review,* lxxxi, 1937, pp. 183–186.

7. Two examples are in the Victoria and Albert Museum (C. 788–1925, a plate, and C. 295–1926, a bottle), and neither is in any respect superior to other English artistic pottery of that time.

8. Nikolaus Pevsner, "Arthur H. Mackmurdo," *The Architectural Review,* lxxxiii, 1938, pp. 141–143.

9. Sir Reginald Blomfield, *Richard Norman Shaw, R. A.,* London, 1940; Nikolaus Pevsner, "Richard Norman Shaw, 1831–1912," *The Architectural Review,* lxxxix, 1941, pp. 41–46.

10. Henry-Russell Hitchcock, Jr., *The Architecture of H. H. Richardson and His Times,* New York, The Museum of Modern Art, 1936.

11. *A Monograph of the Work of McKim, Mead and White, 1879–1915,* New York [1915–1919] vol. i, *1879–1898.*

3. *Eighteen-ninety in Painting*

1. Ambroise Vollard, *Renoir, an Intimate Record.* New York, 1925, p. 129.

2. Joachim Gasquet, *Cézanne,* Paris, 1921, p. 46.

3. Paul Cézanne, *Letters,* London [1941] p. 234.

4. Vincent van Gogh, *Letters to Emile Bernard.* New York, The Museum of Modern Art, 1938, p. 51.

5. *Further Letters of Vincent van Gogh to his Brother. 1886–1889,* London, 1929, p. 174.

6. *Ibid.,* p. 171.

7. *Ibid.,* p. 166. It is interesting to see that certain remarks of Cézanne point to the same idea. He refused to paint Clemenceau because he could not help imagining "bitter blue and poisonous yellow" and "convulsive lines" as soon as he began thinking of him. He accounts for this by saying: "This man does not believe in God." Gasquet, *op. cit.,* p. 118.

8. *Further Letters . . .,* p. 384.

9. *Ibid.,* pp. 332, 413.

10. *Ibid.,* p. 203.

11. Cf. Charles Fegdal, *Félix Vallotton,* Paris, 1931.

12. Cf. Jean Louis Sponsel, *Das moderne Plakat,* Dresden, 1897; Charles Matlack Price, *Posters,* New York, 1913; E. McKnight Kauffer, *The Art of the Poster,* London, 1924.

4. *Art Nouveau*

1. See his decoration of a porch and staircase at Chalfont St. Peter of 1888. Illustrated in *The British Architect,* xxxiii, 1890, pp. 26–27.

2. Cf. *The Early Work of Aubrey Beardsley,* London, 1899, and *The Later Work of Aubrey Beardsley,* London, 1901.

3. Yet he may still have been impressed even at that time by some such works of Rossetti as the wood engravings to Moxon's edition of Tennyson's *Poems* (London, 1857) — especially *The Lady of Shalott,* p. 75, and *The Palace of Art,* p. 113.

4. A third should probably be added to them: Antonio Gaudí (1852–1926). But he remained from the beginning of his career to his very death so much of an outsider, with a background so different from that of any of the other pioneers of the late 19th century, and a development in so different a direction from that taken by the Modern Movement, that one remains embarrassed wherever one tries to allot him a historical place. Yet it is an undeniable fact that his ornamental ironwork of such houses as *El Capricho* at Comillas of 1883–85, and the Güell house at Barcelona of 1885–89 (right) is every bit as surprising and original as Mackmurdo's and Sullivan's and also every bit as close to *Art Nouveau*. But it forms part of buildings in a crazy Pyrenean historicism of medieval and Baroque derivation. The frenzy of Gaudí's style grew more and more baffling with the slow growth of the church of the *Sagrada Familia*, although it can now perhaps be recognized that it bridges the whole distance from the historicism of the late 19th century to that Expressionism of 1920 to which we shall come back for a moment at the end of this chapter. For Gaudí see: Josep F. Ràfols, *Antoni Gaudí* [Barcelona] 1928; for the Church of the *Sagrada Familia*: I. Puig Boada, *El Temple de la Sagrada Familia*, Barcelona, 1929.

5. M. le Baron Horta, in a letter to the author, dated January 23, 1936, says that his only intention in designing No. 12 rue de Turin was "de faire œuvre personnelle d'architecte, à l'égale du peintre et du sculpteur qui ne souciaient que de voir avec leurs yeux et sentir avec leur cœur . . .," though at the same time he stresses the rational plan and construction of the house. He adds that Voysey and Beardsley were unknown to him when he created his early works. Toorop he does not mention either in a positive or a negative way.

6. It certainly has not been solved either by Hugh Morrison in his *Louis Sullivan,* New York, the Museum of Modern Art, 1935, or in Henry R. Hope's article, "Louis Sullivan's Architectural Ornament," in the *Magazine of Art,* xl, 1947, pp. 110–117 (reprinted in *The Architectural Review,* cii, 1947, pp. 111–114).

7. Sullivan, *op. cit.,* p. 189.

8. Van de Velde, *Die Renaissance . . .,* p. 61 ff.

9. Ch. Conrady and R. Thibaut, *Paul Hankar,* Edition Texhuc, Revue La Cité, 1923.

10. And incidentally also the connection between his style and the fact that he advocated a reformed "organic" style in women's clothes.

11. How far he was entirely on his own in these innovations cannot yet be said. The author, in his researches into the work of Christopher Dresser (see note 6, Chapter 2), came across photographs of some of Dresser's Clutha glass of between 1880 and 1890 which is oddly similar to Gallé's. One vase is illustrated in *The Architectural Review,* lxxxi, 1937, p. 184. It may be inspired by Gallé or independent of him.

12. *The Art Work of Louis C. Tiffany,* New York, 1914; also a prospectus with illustrations called *Tiffany, Favrile Glass,* 1896.

13. For a contemporary American account see A. D. F.

Gaudí: Güell house, Barcelona. 1885–89. Ornamental ironwork

Hamlin, "L'Art Nouveau, Its Origin and Development," *The Craftsman,* iii, 1902–03, pp. 129–143.

14. Marcus Whiffen, *Stuart and Georgian Churches Outside London,* London [1947–48] pp. 77–78; cf. also John Gloag and Derck Bridgewater, *Cast Iron in Architecture,* London, 1948; Richard Sheppard, *Cast Iron in Building,* London [1945] and J. Summerson *et al. The Official Architect,* viii, 1945, p. 235 ff. On Berlin see H. Schmitz, *Berliner Eisenguss,* Berlin, 1917.

15. Henry-Russell Hitchcock, "London Coal Exchange," *The Architectural Review,* ci, 1947, pp. 185–187.

16. A. D. F. Hamlin in his article of 45 years ago (quoted in note 13) overrated the originality and importance of France. After all, he says himself that as early as 1895 an article came out in Paris pleading for a restoration of the independence of French designers from Belgium. At least one of the leading French representatives of *Art Nouveau* was Belgian himself: Jean Dampt.

17. Van de Velde is wrong in saying (*Die Renaissance . . .,* p. 15) that before the Dresden Exhibition "nobody in Germany had thought of a revival of artistic craftsmanship."

18. For further information cf. Schmalenbach, *op. cit.,* and more recently the personal reminiscences of Friedrich Ahlers-Hestermann, *Stilwende,* Berlin, 1941 and of Karl Scheffler, *Die fetten und die mageren Jahre,* Leipzig, 1946.

19. F. Fendler, special issue of *Berliner Architektur-Welt,* 1901.

20. Cf. Schmalenbach, *op. cit.,* p. 26.

21. Their most eruptive form is the Oertel Monument of 1901–02, illustrated e.g. in Karl Scheffler, *Die Architektur der Grosstadt,* Berlin, 1913, p. 182, and Ahlers-Hestermann, *op. cit.,* p. 63. It should be understood in conjunction with the contemporary ornament of Sullivan on the one hand and of Gaudí on the other.

Berlage: The architect's house on the Oude Schevening-
sche Weg, The Hague. 1898. Stairhall

22. Walter Crane, *William Morris to Whistler*, London,
1911, p. 232.

23. However, it is not in all cases correct to say that the
really creative designers in the *Art Nouveau* fashion found a
way from it into the Modern Movement. There are also a few
very individual examples of artists developing their versions
of *Art Nouveau* direct into that odd and wild architectural
idiom characteristic of the very first years after the First
World War and parallel to Expressionism in German painting.
The examples are Antonio Gaudí in Barcelona (see note 4,
Chapter 4), and in an even more surprising way H. P. Berlage
in Amsterdam. Gaudí had taken his inspiration ever since the
nineties from the Catalan Middle Ages, the Spanish Baroque
and Indian architecture, and now proceeded to mix them up
into a frantic concoction possible only in the country of
Churriguera. Gaudí's Church of the *Sagrada Familia* will no
doubt remain as an anachronistic monument to the eternal
Southern Baroque. In Berlage there is nothing southern or
luxurious. His historical sources were the Northern brick
forms of the late Middle Ages, sober, sound, and severe. Yet
in his most famous building, the Exchange at Amsterdam of
1898, and even more in his own house in the Oude Sche-
veningsche Weg at The Hague which also dates from 1898
(above), he invented curious jagged and spiky ornamental
forms, not sinuous as those of Gaudí and *Art Nouveau*, but
just as original and daring. These were then exaggerated into
a completely fantastic style by such architects as van der Mey
(Shipping Building, Amsterdam, 1912) and de Klerck —
and from there a straight path leads to Dudok and the nine-
teen-twenties. On Berlage see K. P. C. de Bazel *et al., Dr.
H. P. Berlage en zijn Werk*, Rotterdam, 1916; J. Havelaer, *Dr.
H. P. Berlage*, Amsterdam [1927]

24. A curious and esthetically most attractive illustration of
this inconsistency is the vignette from C. R. Ashbee's first
book (opposite). The book is called *A Few Chapters on Workshop Reconstruction and Citizenship* and came out in London
in 1894. It deals with the social necessity of reintroducing
craft and fighting the evils of modern civilization. Yet Ashbee
the artist contradicts in visual terms Ashbee the reformer. The
smoke from the factory chimney rises in such pretty *Art
Nouveau* curves, the black soot from the clouds descends so
daintily, and the anachronistic barge with her wind-filled
sails answers so sensitively the sweep of the coast line that all
reforming zeal is lulled into esthetic satisfaction.

25. A similar change of trend about that time is to be
noticed in the German periodical *Innendekoration*. This journal was started by Alexander Koch (1860–1939) in 1890.
Whereas the first years are entirely concerned with period
decoration, there are in 1894 some few illustrations of work of
Ernest Newton's and George & Peto's, and also of English
wallpapers printed by Jeffrey's and Essex'. From 1895 on.
forms of *Art Nouveau* begin to penetrate. In 1896, Alexander
Koch added to the *Innendekoration* his *Deutsche Kunst und
Dekoration*. The victory of the new style in the *Innendekoration* is marked by Koch's publication of Baillie Scott's and
Ashbee's rooms for the palace at Darmstadt. He was largely
co-responsible for the foundation of that colony of artists at
the Darmstadt Court which is mentioned on page 119. Ernst
Michalski, whose article on the Jugendstil ("Die entwick-
lungsgeschichtliche Bedeutung des Jugendstils," *Repertorium
für Kunstwissenschaft*, xlvi, 1925, pp. 133–149) is a most
constructive contribution to the solution of the problems of
Art Nouveau, was kind enough to examine for me the volumes
of *Innendekoration*.

26. Maus, *op. cit.*

5. *Engineering and Architecture in the Nine-teenth Century*

1. But in the author's opinion no more potent. It is the one
objection to Sigfried Giedion's brilliant *Space, Time and
Architecture*, Cambridge, Mass., 1941, that it somewhat over-
emphasizes the technical as against the esthetic components of
the modern style.

2. Since this book was first published in 1936, our knowledge of iron in architecture has been greatly increased by the
relevant chapters of Giedion's book mentioned in the previous
note. They amplify considerably what Dr. Giedion had compiled for his *Bauen in Frankreich, Eisen, Eisenbeton*, Leipzig
[1928] a book in its turn clearly dependent on Alfred Gott-
hold Meyer's *Eisenbauten*, Esslingen, 1907. An important
paper was published by S. B. Hamilton, "The Use of Cast Iron
in Building," in *Transactions of the Newcomen Society*, xxi,
1940–41, pp. 139–155. The following account repeats much
that is contained in these publications, but readers familiar
with them will notice where additional information has been

incorporated. Such information refers chiefly to Britain which, on the whole, is not paid quite as much attention by Dr. Giedion as she might be. Research now in progress will prove that. See also the recent books quoted in note 14, Chapter 4.

3. T. Telford, *An Account of the Improvements of the Port of London,* London, 1801, p. 6.

4. *The Architectural Review,* xciii, 1943, pp. 53, 55.

5. Hamilton, *loc. cit.,* p. 141; Alfred von Wolzogen, *Aus Schinkels Nachlass,* Berlin, 1862–64, iii, p. 141.

6. To Charles E. Peterson, architect of the National Park Service, should go great credit for the early recognition of the importance of these buildings. It was largely due to his efforts that the most important of these buildings were preserved, and he has long fought for local and national recognition of their merit. Cf. his "A Museum of American Architecture," *The Octagon,* Nov. 1936; *idem,* "The Museum of American Architecture: A Progress Report," *Journal of the American Society of Architectural Historians,* i, 1941, pp. 24–26.

7. Mentioned by Talbot Hamlin, *Greek Revival Architecture in America,* Oxford University Press, 1944, p. 150.

8. Lecture to the Royal Institute of British Architects, February 29, 1864, quoted from Thomas Harris, *The Three Periods of English Architecture,* London, 1894, p. 84. Aitchison built, for example, No. 59–61 Mark Lane in London in 1863. Professor Hitchcock's paper on the Glasgow warehouse will appear in the *Architectural Review.*

9. *The British Architect,* xxxvii, 1892, p. 347.

10. *The Builder,* xxiii, 1865, p. 296.

Ashbee: Book cover. 1894

11. On the Tees bridge: W. Hutchinson, *History and Antiquities of the County Palatine of Durham,* iii, p. 279. On the Jacob's Creek bridge: James Finley, "A Description of the Patent Chain Bridge," *The Port Folio,* n.s. iii, 1810, pp. 441–453.

12. A cast-iron obelisk earlier than Wilkinson's exists at Ullersdorf in Silesia. Its date is 1802 and it is 72 feet high (see Schmitz, *op. cit.,* p. 19). The philosopher Fichte received another as a monument in 1814. Iron *flêches* became quite usual in the 19th century, see for instance the Cathedrals of Rouen and of Notre Dame in Paris.

13. Whiffen, *op. cit.,* p. 53, plate 67. Dr. Giedion, *Space, Time and Architecture,* fig. 59, p. 120, has illustrated a London bookshop with undisguised iron shafts supporting a little dome. The date is 1794.

14. On Covent Garden: J. Britton and A. Pugin, *Illustrations of the Public Buildings of London,* London, 1825–28, i, p. 220, plate VI; on the Liverpool iron churches see A. T. Brown, *How Gothic Came Back to Liverpool,* University of Liverpool Press, 1937; on John Cragg: J. Nasmyth's *Autobiography,* London, 1883, p. 183. Nasmyth speaks of St. James', Liverpool, as an iron church by Blore. It has not been possible to verify this. Mr. Whiffen's notes (*Stuart and Georgian Churches*) are headed by a reference to Tetbury, Gloucestershire, of 1777–81. However, the vicar has since denied in a letter that the slim piers have iron cores. So Everton may well be the first instance of main piers of iron.

15. *The Works of Sir John Soane,* Sir John Soane Museum Publication No. 8 [London, 1923] p. 91.

16. For these as well as other examples of early 19th century cast iron see: R. Sheppard, *Cast Iron in Building,* London, 1945, and John Summerson *et al.* in *Official Architect,* May, 1945.

17. Humphry Repton in his book of 1808 called *Designs for the Pavilion* (Loudon's edition 1840, p. 391) already recommended cast iron as "peculiarly adapted to some light parts of the Indian style." However, it may be that Nash was preceded by James Wyatt, his closest competitor. At least it is said that Wyatt's ill-fated new palace at Kew, begun in 1802, carried on until 1811, but never completed, was constructed entirely of iron with the exception of the floor boards. See: Antony Dale, *James Wyatt,* Oxford, 1936, p. 98. There is indeed an interesting patent of 1800 for "arched ceilings of cast iron [supported] by hollow pillars, cylinders, tubes, or pipes of the same material" (Patent Office, London, 1800, No. 2410), but it was taken by Samuel Wyatt, James' brother, and in any case the palace was begun too early for the use of a patent of 1800. So Mr. Dale's story may not be correct. It is, incidentally, not confirmed by the captions to any of the existing old illustrations of the castellated palace.

18. Sir G. S. Mackenzie, "On the Form which the Glass of a Forcing-House ought to have, in order to receive the greatest possible Quantity of Rays from the Sun," *Transactions of the Horticultural Society of London,* ii, 1818, pp. 170–177; Thomas Andrew Knight, "Upon the Advantages and Disadvantages of Curvilinear Iron Roofs to Hot-Houses," *Transactions of the Horticultural Society of London,* v, 1824, pp. 227–

Brewer: Exhibition stand for Heal's, Paris Exhibition. 1900

233; J. C. Loudon, *Remarks on the Construction of Hothouses,* London, 1817; *idem, Sketches of Curvilinear Hothouses,* London, 1818; *idem, Encyclopaedia of Gardening,* London, 1822, No. 6174; *idem, Encyclopaedia of Cottage, Farm and Villa Architecture and Furniture,* London, 1842, figure 1732.

19. On railway architecture the standard work is now Carroll L. V. Meeks, *The Architectural Development of the American Railway Station,* unpublished dissertation presented to the Faculty in Architecture at Harvard University, 1948. Professor Meeks compares these wide spans with the largest stone spans ever achieved, notably the Pantheon in Rome 142 feet, Florence Cathedral 138 feet, St. Peter's in Rome 137 feet, St. Paul's in London 112 feet, St. Sophia in Constantinople 107 feet, etc.

20. T. Harris, "What is Architecture?" *Examples of the Architecture of the Victorian Age,* London, 1862, p. 57. Peter F. R. Donner in "A Harris Florilegium," *The Architectural Review,* xciii, 1943, pp. 53–54, suggested that Harris was also the editor of this volume, which was to be the first of a series but of which only this one appeared.

21. John Ruskin, *The Seven Lamps of Architecture,* New York, 1849, p. 33; *idem, The Stones of Venice,* New York [1851] i, pp. 407, 405.

22. Sir George Gilbert Scott, *Remarks on Secular and Domestic Architecture,* London, 1858, pp. 109–110.

23. Viollet-le-Duc, *Entretiens sur l'architecture,* Paris, 1863–72, quoted from the English translation, *Discourses on Architecture,* Boston, 1875–81, ii, pp. 53, 89, 44.

24. Also at Vésinet (Seine-et-Oise) in 1863 and at Notre Dame de France off Leicester Square in London in 1868 (see *The Builder,* xxiii, 1865, pp. 800, 805, and *The Architectural Review,* ci, 1947, p. 111).

25. Not Cottancin as in Gustav Adolf Platz, *Die Baukunst der Neuesten Zeit,* 2nd ed., Berlin [1930] and in Giedion's books quoted above.

26. Summed up most succinctly in the mimeographed catalog *Early Modern Architecture, Chicago, 1870–1910,* 2nd ed., New York, The Museum of Modern Art, 1940. Cf. also Giedion, *Space, Time and Architecture,* and Thomas E. Tallmadge, *Architecture in Old Chicago,* Chicago [1941]

27. L. S. Buffington's dreams of cloud-scrapers of 1880–81 were based on Viollet-le-Duc's *Entretiens* and remained vague. He did not take his patent until 1888 by which time the first Chicago skyscrapers were already in existence. Cf. Hugh Morrison, "Buffington and the Invention of the Skyscraper," *Art Bulletin,* xxvi, 1944, pp. 1–2; Dimitros Tselos, "The Enigma of Buffington's Skyscraper," *Art Bulletin,* xxvi, 1944, pp. 3–12; Muriel B. Christison, "How Buffington Staked His Claim," *Art Bulletin,* xxvi, 1944, pp. 13–24; *The Origin of the Skyscraper,* Report of the Committee appointed by the Trustees of the Estate of Marshall Field for the Examination of the Structure of the Home Insurance Building, Thomas E. Tallmadge, ed., Chicago, 1939.

28. Louis H. Sullivan, "The Tall Office Building Artistically Considered," *Lippincott's Monthly Magazine,* lvii, 1896, p. 405.

29. Houses were built of concrete in America as early as the 1840's and '50's. Cf. Walter L. Creese, "Fowler and the Domestic Octagon," *The Art Bulletin,* xxviii, 1946, pp. 89–102.

30. Ruskin, *The Stones of Venice,* p. 406.

6. *England, Eighteen-ninety to Nineteen-fourteen*

1. There is as yet no book in existence on Voysey, and the only recent paper on his work is not very detailed: Nikolaus Pevsner, "Charles F. Annesley Voysey," *Elsevier's Maandschrift,* 1940, pp. 343–355. The same author has compiled a catalog of Voysey's oeuvre as an architect, and of this a typewritten copy is kept at the Royal Institute of British Architects. For earlier publications of Voysey's work cf. *Dekorative Kunst,* i, 1898, p. 241 ff., and H. Muthesius, *Das englische Haus,* Berlin, 1904–05, i, p. 162 ff.

2. The clearest proof of this influence of Voysey's is Adolphe Crespin's wallpapers, designed at Brussels in the nineties. *Art et décoration,* ii, 1897, p. 92 ff.

3. *The Studio,* i, 1893, p. 234.

4. On the Japanese influence in the sixties see for instance John Rewald, *The History of Impressionism,* New York, The Museum of Modern Art [1946] p. 176.

5. The Peacock Room now at the Freer Gallery of Art in Washington was decorated by Whistler in 1876–77; the *Princesse* had been painted in 1863–64. Japanese woodcuts had become known owing to a chance discovery by Braque-

mond, the etcher, in Paris in 1856. He introduced them to the Goncourts, to Baudelaire, Manet, Degas. Whistler must have first seen examples when he studied in Paris between 1855 and 1859.

6. E. R. and J. Pennell, *The Life of J. McN. Whistler,* London, 1908, i, p. 219. The exhibitions for which he was responsible in 1883 and 1884 had white and lemon yellow, and white and pink walls (pp. 310 and 313).

7. Two more interesting instances of this confusion between old — *i.e.* "L'Art pour l'Art" outlook — and new ideas are the passage from Théophile Gautier, quoted on pages 76–77 and that from Oscar Wilde quoted on page 12. See also Felix M. Gatz, "Die Theorie des l'art pour l'art und Théophile Gautier," *Zeitschrift für Aesthetik und allgemeine Kunstwissenschaft,* vol. 29, 1935, pp. 116–140.

8. Morris speaks of the "impression on a very shortsighted person of divers ugly incidents seen through the medium of a London fog," National Association for the Advancement of Art and its Application to Industry, *Transactions, Edinburgh Meeting, 1889,* London, 1890, p. 199.

9. *Ernest Gimson, His Life and Work,* Stratford-on-Avon, 1924.

10. Sir Lawrence Weaver, "Tradition and Modernity in Craftsmanship," *The Architectural Review,* lxiii, 1928, pp. 247–249.

11. First illustrations in *The Studio,* v, 1895. Cf. also M. H. Baillie Scott, *Houses and Gardens,* London, 1906.

12. The Magpie and Stump, their righthand neighbor, was built earlier and is much less interesting. (Illustrated in *The Studio,* v, 1895, p. 66.)

13. One of Brewer's most charming designs was the exhibition stand for Heal's at the Paris Exhibition of 1900 (illustrated on opposite page).

14. The same arch appears already in Townsend's early work, the Bishopsgate Institute in London of 1892–94. Its connection with Richardson was spotted by P. F. R. Donner, "Treasure Hunt," *The Architectural Review,* xci, 1941, pp. 23–25.

15. Since so much has been said and written about him during the last few years, and yet so little exact information can be obtained, it may be useful to print here as much as I was able to collect in Glasgow. In collecting this, I received much valuable help from Mr. A. G. Henderson, Mr. John Keppie, Mr. W. Davidson and Professor A. Mainds.

A Mackintosh Bibliography exists at the Mitchell Library. Among publications, it is sufficient to mention the following: H. Muthesius, *Haus eines Kunstfreundes,* Darmstadt, 1902; Desmond Chapman-Huston, "Charles Rennie Mackintosh," *Artwork,* vi, 1930, pp. 19–31; E. A. Taylor, "A Neglected Genius, C. R. Mackintosh," *The Studio,* cv, 1933, pp. 345–352; P. Morton Shand, "Glasgow Interlude," *The Architectural Review,* lxxvii, 1935, pp. 23–26. Thieme-Becker's *Künstlerlexikon* does not include Mackintosh's name at all.

Dates (provided by Messrs. Keppie and Henderson, unless another source is mentioned in parentheses): Born June 7, 1868 (letter from the late W. Davidson to the author). Entered the Glasgow School of Art in 1885, at the age of 16

Mackintosh: *Glasgow Herald* Tower. 1894

(Chapman-Huston). In 1887 he was articled to J. Hutchison (Chapman-Huston). In 1889 he joined the firm of John Honeyman and Keppie as a draftsman. He became a partner in 1904 and left the firm in 1913. In 1890 he won a traveling scholarship to France and Italy (Chapman-Huston). His Soane Medallion drawings were published by *The British Architect,* xxxvii, 1892, following p. 174. His design for the *Glasgow Herald* Tower (above) is supposed to date from 1893 (Chapman-Huston), when he was still employed by Honeyman and Keppie (*The British Architect,* xliii, 1895, p. 96). The next illustrations of his work: *The British Architect,* xliv, 1895, p. 14 has the Bargemen's Institute at Dundas by Honeyman and Keppie, with a decorative detail such as the clock face probably done by Mackintosh. The Honeyman and Keppie design for the Glasgow University, Queen Margaret College Medical Department, includes a drawing signed by Mackintosh, *The British Architect,* xlv, 1896, pp. 26–27. Meanwhile *The Studio* had discovered Mackintosh and shown a settee by him in 1896 (vol. ix, p. 205). In 1897 (vol. xi) the same magazine brought out the first special article on Mackintosh, with several illustrations: Gleeson White, "Some Glasgow Designers and Their Work," pp. 86–100; 227–236. The earliest

Creswell: Queensferry Factory, near Chester, England. 1901

19. What else is of interest in England between 1900 and 1914 as heralding the Modern Movement has been collected by the author in an article, "Nine Swallows — No Summer," *The Architectural Review*, xci, 1942, pp. 109–112. The most noteworthy buildings are H. B. Creswell's Queensferry Factory of 1901 (left) and Lethaby's Eagle Insurance in Birmingham of 1900.

20. P. 12 and note 33, Chapter 1.

21. Nikolaus Pevsner, "Model Houses for the Labouring Classes," *The Architectural Review*, xciii, 1943, pp. 119–128.

22. J. M. Richards, "Sir Titus Salt," *The Architectural Review*, lxxx, 1936, pp. 213–218.

23. Cf. Werner Hegemann, *Der Städtebau*, Berlin, 1911–13, 2 vols. With regard to the outstanding position of Germany in pre-war town planning H. Inigo Triggs writes in his *Town Planning, Past, Present and Possible*, London [1909] p. 39: "Nowhere has the subject of town planning received more careful attention than in Germany, where for many years the foremost architects of the country have given much thought to the subject, and where the State practically compels municipalities to own land for public improvement. . . ."

foreign articles were *Dekorative Kunst,* iii, 1899, pp. 48–49, and *Ver Sacrum,* iii, 1900, pp. 384–385, and iv, 1901, pp. 393–408. The foundation stone of the Glasgow School of Art was laid in 1898 and the east half of the building in Renfrew Street opened in 1899. Cranston Tea Room, Buchanan Street, 1897–98; Design *Daily Record* Offices, 1900; Design House for a German Art Collector, 1901 (Muthesius); Gate Lodge, Auchinbothie, Kilmacolm, 1901; Music Room for Fr. Werndorfer, 1901–02; House for Dr. Blackie, Helensburgh, 1902; House for W. Davidson, Windyhill, Kilmacolm, 1903; Cranston Tea Room, Sauchiehall Street (almost entirely destroyed), 1903 and 1906; House for J. Cochrane, Houshill, Nitshill, 1904; Scotland Street School, 1904; House for F. J. Shand, Killearn, 1906; Cranston Tea Room, Argyle Street, 1905; Cottage for H. B. Collins, Auchinbothie, Kilmacolm, 1907; Cranston Tea Room, Ingram Street, 1907, 1909, 1911; Art School, West Wing, 1907–09 (not 1894 as stated in caption to plate facing p. 185, *The Architectural Review,* lxxiii, 1933).

16. Cf. Thomas Howarth, "Mackintosh and the Scottish Tradition," *Magazine of Art,* xli, 1948, pp. 264–267.

17. A wall of the exhibition is illustrated in Ahlers-Hestermann, *op. cit.,* p. 98. On the other hand, the paintings which Mackintosh created in his later years seem to reflect the manner which was developed by Klimt's pupils, especially E. Schiele, during the first years of our century.

18. Mrs. J. R. Newbury, in the introduction to the catalog of the Glasgow Memorial Exhibition, also gives the names of Beardsley, Toorop and Voysey, and adds that of Carlos Schwabe. Toorop's *The Three Brides* was illustrated in *The Studio,* i, 1893, p. 247.

7. *The Modern Movement before Nineteen-fourteen*

1. On Perret see Paul Jamot, *A.-G. Perret et l'architecture du béton arme*, Paris, 1927; on Garnier see Giulia Veronesi, *Tony Garnier*, Milan, 1948.

2. Tony Garnier, *Une Cité Industrielle,* Paris [1918]

3. Le Corbusier and P. Jeanneret, *Ihr Gesamtes Werk von 1910–1929,* Zurich, 1930.

4. Le Corbusier, *Towards a New Architecture,* London, 1931, pp. 80, 82. Also *The Architectural Review,* lxxvi, 1934, p. 41.

5. And how little on Roger Fry's Omega Workshops, started in 1912, has really been brought out by Nikolaus Pevsner, "Ω," *The Architectural Review,* xc, 1941, pp. 45–48.

6. The standard work on Frank Lloyd Wright is Henry-Russell Hitchcock, *In the Nature of Materials,* New York, 1942.

7. *Ausgeführte Bauten und Entwürfe von Frank Lloyd Wright* [Berlin, Wasmuth, 1910] and *Frank Lloyd Wright: Ausgeführte Bauten* (with an introduction by C. R. Ashbee), Berlin, Wasmuth, 1911. These two publications were followed by two written by Dutchmen: H. T. Wijdeveld, *The Life-Work of the American Architect Frank Lloyd Wright,* 7 special numbers of *Wendingen,* 1925, and H. de Fries, *Frank Lloyd Wright,* Berlin, 1926. After that there came two French books, one of them with an introduction by Henry-Russell Hitchcock. America followed very much later. The most striking example of Wright's influence on Holland is a house by van 't Hoff of 1915, illustrated with a few other Wrightian

Sant' Elia: Design for a *City of the Future*. 1913

buildings in Europe by Nikolaus Pevsner, "Frank Lloyd Wright's Peaceful Penetration of Europe," *The Architects' Journal,* lxxxix, 1939, pp. 731–734.

8. The only noteworthy Italian contribution to the new style before the war is the plan for a *Città Futura* designed in 1914 by the futurist Antonio Sant' Elia (1888–1916). The fantastic group of skyscrapers illustrated above is particularly interesting because of the bold use made of the motif of receding stories, although it is likely that Sant' Elia developed this idea under the influence of Garnier's and Perret's works. Equally interesting is his manifesto on futurist architecture which he wrote in 1914. Here he says: "The architecture of Futurism is the architecture of calculation, of boldness, and of simplicity, the architecture of concrete, iron, glass . . . and all the new synthetic materials replacing wood, stone, brick which enable us to obtain a maximum of elasticity and lightness." See Alberto Sartoris, *Sant' Elia e l'architettura futurista,* Rome, 1943; Giulio Carlo Argan, "Il Pensiero critico di Antonio Da Sant' Elia," *L'Arte,* xxxiii, 1930, pp. 491–498; *Emporium,* xlv, 1917, pp. 155–159; and Giulio Carlo Argan *et al., Dopo Sant' Elia,* Milan, 1935, where the Manifesto is reprinted, pp. 9–15.

9. A. Endell, "Formenschönheit und Dekorative Kunst," *Dekorative Kunst,* ii, p. 121 ff.

10. J. A. Lux, *Josef Maria Olbrich,* Vienna, 1919.

11. But there once again Sullivan had come first. Olbrich's block with its semi-spheric dome and Olbrich's sense of flat vegetal decoration already appear in Sullivan's Wainwright Tomb, Bellefontaine Cemetery, St. Louis, in 1892. Illustrated in Hugh Morrison, *op. cit.,* plate 41.

12. Leopold Kleiner, *Josef Hoffmann,* Berlin [1927] also *Wendingen,* no. 8–9, 1920.

13. Heinrich Kulka, *Adolf Loos; das Werk des Architekten,* Vienna, 1931.

14. Cf., for example, the house built by Peter Behrens at Northampton in 1926; illustrated in *The Architectural Review,* lx, 1926, p. 177.

15. Fritz Hoeber, *Peter Behrens,* Munich, 1913, and Paul Joseph Cremers, *Peter Behrens, sein Werk von 1909 bis zur Gegenwart,* Essen [1928]

16. Illustrated in *The Architectural Review,* lxxvi, 1934, p. 40.

17. Cf. Schmalenbach, *op. cit.,* pp. 28–29, 85.

18. On this see Ahlers-Hestermann, *op. cit.,* p. 109.

19. Joseph Popp, *Bruno Paul,* Munich, n.d.

20. Illustrated *ibid.,* p. 31 ff., and *Dekorative Kunst,* xviii, 1909, p. 191 ff.

21. Philip C. Johnson, *Mies van der Rohe,* New York, The Museum of Modern Art [1947]

22. Theodor Heuss, *Hans Poelzig,* Berlin, 1939.

23. See Paul Mebes, *Um 1800,* Munich, 1920, and Fritz Stahl, *Karl Friedrich Schinkel,* Berlin [1911]

24. And as Octave Mirbeau had visualized it as early as 1889. His term is "combinaisons aériennes" (Giedion, *Bauen in Frankreich,* p. 18).

Table of Names and Dates

Born	Architects and Designers	Painters
1750–1830	Telford 1757–1834	
	Finley ?–1828	
	Paxton 1801–65	
	Horeau 1801–72	
	Labrouste 1801–75	
	Brunel 1806–59	
	Boileau 1812–96	
		Moreau 1826–98
1830–40	Shaw 1831–1912	Rossetti 1828–82
	Webb 1831–1915	
	Jenney 1832–1907	
	Eiffel 1832–1923	
	Morris 1834–96	Burne-Jones 1833–98
	Dresser 1834–1904	Whistler 1834–1923
	de Baudot 1834–1915	
	Nesfield 1835–88	
	Richardson 1838–86	
1840–50	Contamin 1840–93	Cézanne 1839–1906
	Selmersheim 1840–1916	Redon 1840–1916
	Wagner 1841–1918	
	Dutert 1845–1906	Rousseau 1844–1910
	Crane 1845–1915	
	Gallé 1846–1904	
	Tiffany 1848–1933	Gauguin 1848–1903
1850–60	Root 1850–91	
	Sullivan 1850–1924	
	Townsend 1850–1928	
	Mackmurdo 1851–1942	
	Gaudí 1852–1926	
	White 1853–1906	

Born	Architects and Designers	Painters
	Messel 1853–1909	van Gogh 1853–90
	Daum 1854–1909	Hodler 1853–1918
	Holabird 1854–1923	
	Roche 1855–1927	
	Berlage 1856–1934	
	Voysey 1857–1941	
	Delaherche 1857–	
	Hankar 1859–1901	Khnopff 1858–1921
	Majorelle 1859–1926	Seurat 1859–91
1860–70		Toorop 1859–1928
		Ensor 1860–
	Muthesius 1861–1927	
	Plumet 1861–1928	
	Horta 1861–1947	Klimt 1862–1918
	Obrist 1863–1927	Munch 1863–1944
	Ashbee 1863–1942	
	van de Velde 1863–	
	Gimson 1864–1920	
	Eckmann 1865–1902	
	Baillie Scott 1865–1945	Vallotton 1865–1925
	Smith 1866–1933	
	Olbrich 1867–1908	Kandinsky 1866–1944
	Guimard 1867–1942	Nolde 1867–
	Brangwyn 1867–	
	Mackintosh 1868–1928	
	Behrens 1868–1940	
	Poelzig 1869–1948	
	Garnier 1869–1948	
	Wright 1869–	
1870–80	Loos 1870–1933	
	Hoffmann 1870–	
	Brewer 1871–1918	
	Endell 1871–1925	
	Heal 1872–	Beardsley 1872·98
	Perret 1874–	
	Paul 1874–	
	Schröder 1878–	
1880–90	Gropius 1883–	
	Mies van der Rohe 1886–	
	Sant' Elia 1888–1917	

147

Sources of Illustrations

pl. 8: Courtesy Victoria and Albert Museum, London

pl. 11: Lethaby, *Philip Webb and His Work,* Oxford University Press, Oxford

pl. 12: Courtesy Bedford Lemere & Co. Ltd., Croydon

pl. 18: Berenice Abbott, New York

pls. 40, 99, 100: Courtesy Chicago Architectural Photographing Co.

pl. 44: Courtesy David Royter, New York

pl. 45: Courtesy Hans van Nes, New York

pl. 54a: Courtesy West Midland Photo Services Ltd., Shrewsbury, England

pl. 61: Chevojon Frères, Paris

pl. 85: Annan, Glasgow

pl. 103: Courtesy Henry-Russell Hitchcock

pl. 115: Kulka, *Adolf Loos,* Anton Schroll & Co., Vienna

p. 139: Courtesy Ampliaciones y Reproducciones Mas, Barcelona

p. 142: Courtesy Heal & Son Ltd., London

Index

This book has been printed in April, 1957 for the Trustees of the Museum of Modern Art, New York by Connecticut Printers, Inc., Hartford, Conn.